Beyond Command and Control: The Strategic Management of Police Departments

Mark H. Moore
Darrel W. Stephens

This paper is published by PERF as a service to its members and the general public. The opinions and recommendations expressed in this paper are those of the authors and do not necessarily represent those of the PERF membership. This paper was made possible by the support of the Ford Foundation.

Table of Contents

Chapter 1

Chapter 2

DEFINING THE POLICE MISSION   27

Chapter 3

CONSTITUTING POLICE DEPARTMENTS   49

Chapter 4

MANAGING POLICE PERFORMANCE: INTERNAL ORGANIZATION AND CONTROL   67

Chapter 5

LEADERSHIP AND THE FUTURE OF POLICING   105

Foreword

For some time the top executives of business firms have been rethinking what corporate leadership means. Prompted by the need to become more competitive in an economic order that is no longer dominated by the United States and aided by the research of many scholars, corporate leaders have been struggling to clarify their missions, redesign their organizations, motivate their workers and sell their customers.

With only a few exceptions, the leaders of government agencies have stood apart from this trend. Many bureau chiefs see no compelling reason to change: if they can get their budget appropriation and avoid press criticism, all is well. Others would like to change but feel overwhelmed by the obstacles they would have to overcome: civil service rules, interest-group pressures, legislative intervention, court orders and financial stringencies. For reasons of indifference or impracticality, both groups may think that the countless books on "corporate culture" have no lessons in them for public administration.

Mark Moore and Darrel Stephens think otherwise. In this concise, pungent, and realistic essay, they make a strong case for applying to one important kind of government agency—the police—the lessons of strategic management. What is more remarkable, many police executives are listening to that message and applying it. In my thirty years of studying public administration, I am struck by the fact that big-city police departments have been more inclined to change than almost any other kind of agency.

It is not hard to imagine why the police might be open to

change. They are on the grinding edge of almost all of society's domestic problems: crime, drug abuse, truancy and public disorder. They are called upon by citizens to address nearly every ill of urban life—abandoned buildings, rutted streets, unruly teenagers, lost children and unsightly graffiti. But if there is one sure lesson one can draw from the study of any organization, public or private, it is that the mere existence of a problem does not inevitably lead to a constructive solution.

What is needed in addition is sound advice and proven success. For years, Professor Mark Moore has been a source of that advice; while chief of police in Newport News, Virginia, Darrel Stephens has been an example of how to put good advice to practical use. The Police Executive Research Forum (PERF) is one organization—the Police Foundation is another—that has brought together new thinking and practical experience so as to improve the quality of policing in this country.

In this monograph, Moore and Stephens distill into plain language the central lessons of their advice and experience. The result is not a recipe book or set of how-to-do-it lessons; police management is too complex to benefit from standardized formulas or one-size-fits-all solutions. The result, instead, is a stimulating lesson in how to think strategically about leadership. It deserves to be read carefully and considered seriously by every police executive—and, in my opinion, every public admini-strator—here and abroad.

James Q. Wilson
Collins Professor of Management and Public Policy
University of California at Los Angeles

Acknowledgements

Work on this book began when Bill Geller urged us to co-author the organization and management chapter of the International City Management Association (ICMA) police administration text. When our work on that chapter greatly exceeded the space limitations, we decided that it would be worthwhile for PERF to publish an expanded and more detailed discussion of our ideas for strategically managing a police organization. We are grateful to Bill for his enthusiasm and encouragement of this effort. We also appreciate ICMA Director of Publications Barbara Moore's support for the idea.

Most of the thoughts and ideas expressed in the book about police management had the benefit of further development in discussions with the members of the Harvard Executive Session on Policing. We are grateful for what they have taught us during those discussions, and to the National Institute of Justice for their support of the Executive Sessions.

We are indebted to members of the PERF staff who made substantial contributions to the publication of this book. Martha Plotkin has the overall responsibility for our publications. Somehow she makes sure that everything in that mysterious process works. Karin Schmerler contributed a great deal to improving each draft with her editorial suggestions and both Steve DeNelsky and Sophia Carr made substantial contributions to the final product.

Darrel W. Stephens
Mark H. Moore

Chapter 1

Police Orthodoxy and Strategic Management

I. THE PREVAILING ORTHODOXY

A powerful orthodoxy rooted in the traditions of military command and scientific management has provided the customary foundation for the theory (and much of the practice) of police management.[1] In this orthodoxy, the mission and goals of police departments are established externally — by law, by formal policy or simply by tradition. The role of police executives is to find efficient means — administrative, programmatic and technological — for achieving those goals. They do so through the traditional managerial functions: planning, organizing, coordinating and controlling.

In planning, police executives translate broad policy goals into specific operational objectives and identify the organizational requirements of those objectives.[2] Planning directs the executives' attention to the organizations' task environment and the demands and challenges of the future. Planning also encourages executives to seek out innovations that will allow their organizations to better deal with old problems, or equip themselves to deal more effectively with problems of the future.

The functions of organizing and coordinating are concerned with the detailed deployment of the organization's resources. A key step is defining the basic structure of the organization.[3] A second is organizing the process of decision making to identify the proper level at which different kinds of decisions can be made, and to ensure that there is some capacity in the organization to identify and resolve important policy questions.[4] Establishing individual accountability and identifying and removing any gaps in the administrative systems that guide individual effort is a third. This includes, for example, maintaining a current manual of policies and procedures, and a complete set of job descriptions defining tasks and responsibilities throughout the organization.

Controlling requires executives to oversee and sanction the conduct of their employees. This includes developing accounting and information systems to keep track of expenditures, activities and accomplishments.[5] It also means developing performance evaluation systems for individual officers and for the organization as a whole.[6] Finally, it includes developing internal investigative and disciplinary procedures to guard against possible abuse of authority.[7]

In addition to these technical functions, police executives are expected to provide inspirational leadership.[8] They must set high standards of ethical conduct for themselves and brook no corruption, malingering or incompetence among their subordinates. In addition, however, they are expected to look after the morale of the organization. Stern discipline must be accompanied by assurances from the executive that those employees who perform well will be rewarded, and that honest mistakes will be reliably distinguished from careless or badly motivated actions. Otherwise, the officers will feel victimized by what they view as arbitrary managerial actions.

As part of exercising leadership, the top managers are also expected to shield their organization from disruptive external pressures – particularly improper political influence. While it is always difficult to distinguish proper political oversight from improper political interference, police executives are expected to resist demands to use the organization's assets for the particular, shortsighted purposes of individual politicians rather than for the broader long-term interests of the citizenry as a whole. These expectations are expressed most often by the employees of the organization, who want to be sure that their leaders will protect the ultimate purposes and values of the organization against arbitrary demands for change.

Taboos of the Traditional Orthodoxy

What the traditional orthodoxy does not expect, much less demand, from police executives is any reconsideration of the basic mission of the organization, or proposals of new ways of using the organization to meet challenges currently facing society. These are matters of policy – not administration or management.

Nor is it considered good form to raise doubts about the efficacy of the organization's current methods for achieving its objectives. While one is expected to adopt those innovations that the field as a whole has certified through operational experience as appropriate, to initiate innovations by oneself is risky. It requires police executives to admit that the current methods may not be the best, and to commit at least some of their organizations to experiments. Both expose police executives to external and

3

internal criticism. To admit to uncertainty is to suggest professional incompetence. To experiment is to show insufficient respect for the accumulated knowledge and traditions of the organization.

Nor is it recommended that managers give their subordinates the discretion to develop their own methods for handling the particular problems they face. Such actions appear to be a retreat from managerial responsibility for setting direction and exercising control. The result of such managerial neglect would, in the focus of the traditional orthodoxy, almost certainly be substantial abuses.

Finally, managers operating under the traditional orthodoxy are not encouraged to use informal channels to obtain advice from local community groups about which problems are important locally. Instead, they must limit themselves to obtaining policy guidance about priorities through central, official channels. Otherwise, they would appear to those inside and outside the organization to be playing politics.

The Challenge to Orthodoxy

This orthodoxy that has long dominated thought about the management of police departments is now being challenged. Although it would probably be an exaggeration to describe the important changes now occurring in police management as a revolution, they certainly constitute a fast-paced evolution. Consider the following points:

- Police executives and scholars are increasingly rais-
  ing basic questions about the mission and goals of
  the police.[9] They no longer see the police mission
  exclusively in terms of crime control. They add crime

prevention, fear reduction, order maintenance, social crisis management and even injury reduction to the basic goal of reducing crime. These goals are added partly to reflect the operational reality that citizens have always relied on the police to perform these functions, and partly because it is increasingly obvious that the police can make important contributions to their communities by performing these functions well.

- Police executives and scholars are increasingly testing the limits of police methods — operational, technological and organizational — and finding them inadequate to the tasks now confronting police agencies. The crime-fighting effectiveness of random and directed patrol, rapid response to calls for service and retrospective criminal investigation now seems less certain than once assumed.[10] For all the emphasis on technology, the police seem to have not yet been able to adapt and fully exploit computer technology for operational and command purposes. And, in a world of limited resources, specialized units that take officers away from general patrol duties seem less obviously valuable than they once did, and the advantages of generalist officers now seem greater.

- Police executives are increasingly experimenting with new internal administrative devices designed to encourage the use of discretion, while ensuring that officers use it effectively and properly. They are relying less on rules and constant supervision and more on selection, training and the articulation of values to create a culture that can properly guide officer conduct.[11]

- Police executives are increasingly wondering whether closer relations with the communities they police might hold the key to improved performance of the organization.[12] They consider this possibility partly because the closer relations will help the police identify what problems are important to solve, partly because the community's own capacities for self-defense might be a key resource to engage in the fight against crime, partly because research has identified the importance of citizens in solving crimes and partly because stronger relations with the community might help police managers hold their organization accountable for its performance.

Toward a New Orthodoxy

The new developments in policing have extremely important implications for the effective organization and management of police departments. Unfortunately, the developments are sufficiently new that their implications have not yet been codified in a new orthodoxy. This monograph takes a first step toward the establishment of that new orthodoxy.

To that end, the remaining sections of Chapter 1 briefly explore the forces that are undermining the orthodoxy in police organization and management and set out a different way of thinking about the organization and management of police departments. This method borrows the concept of corporate strategy from the private sector and adapts it for use in the public sector. Then, in Chapter 2, the concept of corporate strategy is used to help define the goals of policing. Chapter 3 analyzes how the police might usefully think about managing their relations with the external environment. Chapter 4 examines the implications of the discussion for the internal structure and operations of police departments. Finally, Chapter 5 looks to the future, and the requirements for imaginative police leadership.

II. FORCES SHAPING MODERN POLICE MANAGEMENT

Three broad forces are now shaping thought about the effective organization and management of police departments. Perhaps the most urgent are important social and economic changes in the nation's cities that affect both the tasks that the police must perform and the resources available to them.

Environmental Pressures on Tasks and Resources

Simply stated, the nation's cities are becoming larger, ethnically more diverse and, generally speaking, poorer. They are poorer both in the sense that they now include more poor people and in the sense that tax bases and government budgets are shrinking. An important reason for this is a middle-class exodus. As the relatively advantaged move to the suburbs, they leave behind crumbling buildings, weakened public institutions and a residual urban population more sharply divided between rich and poor.[13]

These trends are changing the nature of police work in fundamental ways. First, there is much more of it to do. Reported crimes and calls for service have increased — sometimes dramatically. In many areas, however, spending for public policing has not kept pace.[14] The rest of the criminal justice system is also losing its capacity to handle the cases the police present. In short, the criminal justice system is going bankrupt: it is losing its capacity to punish, deter, incapacitate and rehabilitate. These facts alone would necessitate some rethinking of past police strategies.

More important, however, the tasks themselves seem to be changing. In today's cities, fear — quite apart from actual criminal victimization — is a problem in its own right.[15] It is fear that is forcing people to stay off the streets and to buy guns. Such actions may make individuals feel safer, but they make the city as a whole a more dangerous place. Fear also contributes to driving small businesses to abandon neighborhoods. With them go jobs for teenagers, contributions to civic groups and rallying points for community development activities. Their departure casts doubt on whether it is worth it to those who stay behind to nag one's children to go to school and stay off drugs, to repair one's apartment or to sweep one's streets.[16]

Similarly, the police are now drawn into many social emergencies that could produce violence. In the past, conflicts within families and other intimate social groups were handled by mediating institutions, such as the family, church, neighborhood and school. With the weakening of these institutions, however, the police are being dragged into unaccustomed terrain. They, rather than family and clergy, are asked to mediate potentially violent domestic disputes. They, rather than family and neighbors, must deal with a 14 year-old runaway. They, rather than a sense of honor and public pressure, are called on to force a landlord to provide heat or to compel a tenant to live up to the terms of the lease. Indeed, much of the crime that the police now handle seems to emerge from nagging disputes among people who know one another rather than from predatory attacks by hardened offenders.[17]

These changes are drawing the police more deeply into the social structures of cities. As they are drawn in, important questions arise. Are the fears, disputes and small social emergencies that prompt calls to the police worth handling well or are they distractions from their central mission of remaining ready to deal with more serious predatory crime? Are the skills and capabilities the police have developed the right ones to handle such situations? If not, why are the police, rather than some other agency, getting the calls? What other agencies might more properly and more effectively be tasked with handling these problems? To whom should the police look for guidance on these questions — to their own professional preferences, to their apparent ability to contribute to the resolution of these problems, to the requirements of the law or to the directives of elected officials?

The Revolution in Managerial Thought

A second broad trend affecting police thinking about the organization and management of police departments is the revolution in managerial thought. In the past, good management focused on internal controls. It was assumed that managers faced stable and predictable environments. To the extent the environment was unstable, the task was to improve one's ability to predict what was going to happen so that the organization would be ready to meet the challenge when it appeared. The emphasis was on allocating and using resources for production rather than for service, marketing or customer relations. Internal administration depended on well-defined operational objectives, the creation and utilization of functional specialties, tight operational control and orderliness in organizational development. Ordinarily, the path to improved organizational performance lay in achieving economies of scale and increasingly standardized procedures.

This line of thinking about management has been profoundly upset by three factors: (1) the economic success of the Japanese (who seem to succeed with a profoundly different managerial philosophy),[18] (2) research into the managerial practices of successful private sector organizations in the United States[19] and (3) the growth in the service economy, with its requirements for a sharp focus on the customer's needs and an ability to adapt standard operations to meet those needs. These trends have changed our images of what good management requires. Predictable external environments and planned change have yielded to the necessity of constant innovation to deal with unpredictable changes in market demands, technological opportunities and competitive pressures. Success for organizations seems to lie less in the ability to achieve economies of scale and standardization than in the ability to adapt and innovate.[20] Theories of tight managerial control have been replaced by doctrines of worker participation, quality circles and shared commitment to excellence as the principal devices for motivating organizational performance.[21] The focus on efficient use of resources within the boundaries of the organization has been transformed to an "open-systems view" that emphasizes the links between the organization and its customers, markets and stakeholders.

Obviously, there are important differences between public sector organizations and private business firms. A police department is not a service organization like a restaurant, bank or insurance company. Yet, just as managerial doctrines in the rest of society are influenced by the broad trends, managerial thought within the field of policing has been influenced. Indeed, the changes in managerial thought have encouraged police executives to think not only in terms of how they might achieve well-defined existing objectives, but also how they might best use the assets of their organization to ameliorate the problems facing cities – even when those problems were not part of their initial mandate. They suggest the possibility of decentralizing police organizations and finding means other than tight supervision to motivate and direct the department's employees. They encourage police executives to analyze their customers, markets and competitors to determine where and how the police might alter their performance to make themselves more valuable.

The Evolution of Policing

The third powerful factor affecting thought about police organization and management is the evolution of thought within the police profession itself. The field of policing may have been buffeted and stimulated by the broader social trends, but policing has also been following a logic of its own as it learns from its own experience and develops its own ideas about how best to police the nation's communities.[22]

For the past 40 years policing has been guided by the "reform strategy" of policing. That strategy emphasized crime fighting as the primary task of the police. It relied primarily on the techniques of random and directed patrol, rapid response to calls for service and retrospective criminal investigation as the key means for accomplishing the crime-fighting objectives. It sought to ensure effective discipline and control through elaborate rules and close supervision. And it tried to guarantee fair and impartial enforcement of the laws by insulating the police from political interference. While the pursuit of this strategy has helped to create more lawful, professional and effective police departments, it is now increasingly clear that the police are approaching the limits of this style of policing.

We now know, for example, that random and directed patrol, rapid response to calls for service and retrospective criminal investigation are limited in terms of their potential impact on crime.[23] They turn out to be particularly dependent on the willingness of citizens to help the police detect and solve crimes. Thus, if the police are to improve their crime-fighting capabilities, they must improve their relations with the communities they police.

We now know, too, that fear is an important problem in its own right, and that it is influenced as much by minor instances of disorder as by violent criminal victimization. We also know that fear can be allayed by making the police more personally accessible to citizens.[24] Thus, the police must make themselves more, rather than less, accessible to citizens.

We have long understood that because of the immediate accessibility and general resourcefulness of the police, citizens use the police for many purposes other than crime fighting.[25] Now, however, police are beginning to view what were previously considered nuisance calls as important ways to foster effective relations with the community and as important clues about where serious problems might be brewing.[26]

We have also long known that police officers have a great deal of *de facto* (if not *de jure*) discretion in the performance of their duties.[27] Under the reform strategy of policing, the crucial administrative task was to eliminate or minimize that discretion through extensive written rules and close supervision. Now, the field is beginning to see discretion as providing the police with the opportunity to adapt responses to particular circumstances. Moreover, it is testing different ways of controlling discretion, such as (1) by articulating organizational values and creating organizational cultures to ensure that the proper values are expressed in particular police actions,[28] (2) by routine after-the-fact auditing of cases to learn and to teach what was right and what wrong and (3) by establishing such mechanisms as community surveys, community consultative groups or ombudsmen to allow the community to help police managers supervise and evaluate officer conduct.

The advantages of being insulated from political pressures have long been apparent, but the disadvantages of being cut off from local communities are also now being recognized. The operational effectiveness of the police is weakened not only when citizens do not feel they can rely on the police, but also when the police lack information about what the community regards as important problems to solve. In addition, without a strong link to local communities, the police must base their legitimacy only on law and expertise. That is a much weaker base than one that includes local popular and political support. It is particularly weak if police claims of impartiality, lawfulness and expertise are not widely credited in the community. In that world, the police begin to lose to competition from private self-defense, as a means of ensuring safety and order.

These developments within the field are shaking the past orthodoxy about police organization and management. While it remains clear that the central mission of the police is crime control, it is less clear that this should be the exclusive focus of the police. While it remains clear that the principal means available to the police to accomplish their objectives is law enforcement, it is becoming increasingly apparent that they can contribute other skills to solve particular problems. While it remains clear that it is important for police executives to demand disciplined conduct from their officers, the best administrative means for producing that result now seem less clear than it once did. And, while it remains clear that the police should be insulated from improper political interference, it seems important that they find mechanisms to discover what the citizens want from them to restore public support for the police through increased responsiveness and accountability.

III. THE STRATEGIC MANAGEMENT OF POLICE DEPARTMENTS

With the past orthodoxy undermined, it is difficult to know what conceptual framework should be used to get police organizations on the right track. One answer is to rely on the concept of "corporate strategy" as an analytic tool.[29] That concept has proven useful to private sector executives facing uncertain and demanding environments. Perhaps it could be useful to police executives who now face similar challenges.

The Concept of Corporate Strategy

According to Kenneth Andrews, the development of a corporate strategy in the private sector has to do "with the choice of purpose, the molding of organization identity and character, the unending definition of what needs to be done, and the mobilization of resources for the attainment of goals in the face of aggressive competition or adverse circumstances."[30] R. Edward Freeman makes the point more succinctly: The concept of corporate strategy is "setting some direction for the organization based on an analysis of organizational capabilities and environmental opportunities and threats."[31]

This concept has two eye-opening aspects for those in the public sector. The first is that it is startling to consider "the choice of purpose" as a managerial function. Indeed, the freedom to conceive different missions is, at first, breathtaking. In the public sector, we ordinarily assume that the purposes are established by "policy makers" rather than "managers." Managers are supposed to think about means, not ends.

The second is that, in this methodology, the purposes of the organization are not preset and defined independently of the immediate circumstances. Instead, they are discovered by exploring the "fit" between the opportunities and challenges that the environment presents and the distinctive capabilities of the organization. A "good" goal is one that describes the principal value-creating opportunities that a particular firm, facing a particular environment and endowed with a particular set of capabilities, can exploit. In the public sector, we are unaccustomed to thinking that proper goals might be discovered by locating opportunities for one's organization to make a contribution to the society. We tend to think of organizational missions in the public sector as being fixed and immutable, not as subject to change when a manager spots an opportunity to create additional public value.

The implication of this new perspective for policing, for example, is that police executives would not necessarily assume that their clear, unambiguous mission was to control crime through professional law enforcement. Instead, they would be encouraged to consider how their organization, with its distinctive capabilities, could make the greatest contribution to the communities they police. That shift in perspective fundamentally changes the questions confronting police executives and their calculations of how best to meet their responsibilities. It is one thing for a police executive to consider how the police force might best be deployed to deal with predatory crime. It is quite a different matter for a police executive to consider how he or she might use a large, disciplined force that carries the authority of the state, has access to transportation and is available on instant notice around the clock to make the maximum contribution to the quality of life within the community.

Strategy in the Public Sector

Although this private sector concept produces some potentially useful shifts in perspective when considered in the public sector context, it must also be adapted to fit the special environment that public managers confront. Figure 1 presents a simple diagram that shows how public sector executives might define and test different ideas about their "corporate strategy."

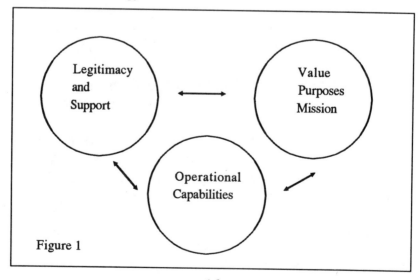

Figure 1

If a particular strategy, or statement of goals and primary means, is to be successful, it must meet the three tests symbolized by the circles in Figure 1.

First, the articulated goals and objectives must describe a purpose that is plausibly valuable to the society. Some public value must be created, some conception of the public interest successfully pursued. Otherwise, the enterprise will be unable to justify its costs. Second, the purpose must be operationally feasible and should take advantage of the distinctive competencies and capabilities of the organization. It must use the organization and its accumulated investments well. Third, the purpose must be able to continue to attract support from those in political and legal positions who authorize the continuation of the enterprise. Otherwise, the enterprise will be ill-founded. If a proposed strategy fails any of these tests — that is, if the proposed purpose has little value to the society, if the proposed purpose cannot be achieved by the organization or if there is little political or legal support for the proposed purpose — then the strategy is not appropriate.

This conception differs from the conception of strategy in the private sector in at least two important respects. First, when one is devising a strategy for a public sector organization, instead of looking at financial returns to the organization, one must pay attention to something that is much harder to define — namely, the public value produced by the organization. To a degree, what constitutes public value is set out in the political and legal mandates governing a public sector enterprise. Thus, for example, the goals of a police force are typically set out in the legislation that established its organizational charter. But there are other means of establishing what is publicly valuable. One can turn, for example, to the techniques of policy analysis to help identify both important social problems to be solved and the means for solving them.[32] One can also turn to program evaluations to determine whether public sector organizations have been effective in achieving purposes set for them.[33] On occasion, one can even use a cost-benefit analysis to determine whether the public is getting its money's worth.[34] Neither the legislative charter nor any of the analyses gives a perfect estimate of what constitutes public value and whether the organization has succeeded in producing it, but the combination of them all may provide some rough guidance.

Second, in formulating a public sector strategy, the attention of the executive is focused not on markets and consumers, but instead on those who grant political and legal authorization for the organization to continue to operate. Instead of focusing on an organization's clients or consumers, the methodology focuses managerial attention on the question of what purposes or aims those in a position to grant the organization a continuing flow of resources will support, and what particular actions would cause the organization to lose credibility with such officials. That piece of the manager's world could be called the "political authorizing environment." It consists of the elected chief executive (usually the mayor), elected representatives to legislative bodies (usually city council members), the heads of administrative oversight agencies such as budget bureaus and civil service commissions, the media, assorted interest groups, the general public and the courts.[35] In this sense, political enthusiasm for the enterprise — built by promises of values to be realized as well as by concrete performance — is the functional analog of market success for private organizations; someone with money to spend continues to buy the product.

This "authorizing environment" supplies something more than money to public sector organizations, however. It also supplies authority for them to compel others to act in the public interest. Indeed, access to public authority is one of the most important differences between private and public sector organizations. In the private sector, money is used to create things of value. In the public sector, laws give public agencies the opportunity to create value by compelling private parties outside the boundaries of their organization to contribute to the public interest. The public agencies that have these powers are responsible for husbanding them and using them only when justified. In this sense, one might think of authorizing committees of legislative bodies and the courts as the agencies that oversee the utilization of public *authority*, just as appropriations committees and budget agencies oversee the use of public *money*. A public sector manager is accountable for the use of authority as well as the use of money. Indeed, it is this fact that puts the courts at the center of the authorizing environment along with political representatives in legislative and executive branch agencies.

The authorizing role of the courts is quite clear in the case of policing and law enforcement. The requirement that the police obtain a search warrant, for example, is a clear example of society's desire to ensure that intrusions on privacy occur only in circumstances in which such intrusions are necessary.[36] The establishment of the exclusionary rule was an effort by the court to make law enforcement organizations comply with rules designed to protect privacy and was prompted by concerns that the police were not taking their obligations to protect privacy seriously enough.[37] One can even view the extensive training that the police undergo in learning about the use of physical force as an effort to minimize its use. Officers who are well-trained in using force, unlike those who are not well-trained, will use the minimal amount of force required in a situation. In short, authority and force are resources granted to police organizations to accomplish public purposes, but police use of these resources is closely observed to ensure that they are used expertly and economically.[38]

In the context of the public sector, therefore, the concept of organizational strategy requires a manager to define purposes of the organization that can sustain political and legal support, are operationally achievable and are plausibly of public value. One can come to a conclusion about such purposes by examining the political and legal demands on the organization, by exploring the task environment that the organization faces and by thinking through the question of how the distinctive competence of an organization might best be utilized. That is the methodology pursued here in reaching conclusions about the effective organization and management of police departments.

A Successful Strategy: "Pollution Abatement" and the EPA

The conclusion of a strategic analysis is a relatively simple phrase that defines the basic mission of an organization.[39] For example, after being appointed Administrator of the United States Environmental Protection Agency (EPA), William Ruckelshaus declared that the basic mission of the organization was "pollution abatement."[40] In the particular institutional environment of the times, that phrase had some important properties.

In substantive terms, the phrase announced how the important social values at stake in environmental protection were to be balanced – at least for a while. In the short run, before society had accumulated real experience with the actual costs and benefits of environmental protection, the government agency acted as though the public interest required moves in the direction of environmental cleanup rather than the protection of economic development at any environmental cost. In a world in which rivers were burning and cities were choked with smog, such a judgment seemed quite plausible even though it was not clear how great the costs of cleanup would be. Nor was it certain whether the most important benefits of environmental cleanup would lie in safer, more attractive or more pristine natural environments.

In political terms, the phrase struck a nice balance between fervent environmentalists frustrated by years of governmental inaction, and those who were concerned about the impact of tight environmental standards on economic growth. To the environmentalists, this account of the EPA's goals suggested action rather than further delay. To businesses, the phrase indicated something less than an all-out war. It also suggested that the effort to control pollution would be an orderly one that focused on the most egregious cases first, and would not reach all businesses until much later – after they had had a chance to adjust. Thus, the conception of the EPA's mission drew grudging support from the key players in Ruckelshaus's authorizing environment.

In operational terms, the phrase pointed toward the key activities that had to be accelerated in the organization and the key organizational capabilities that had to be created.

Specifically, it implied that visible enforcement activities had to be undertaken. This led Ruckelshaus to create a separate Office of Enforcement, with a director reporting directly to him, and to make the filling of that job the highest personnel priority. It also led the organization to plan and carry out a carefully orchestrated set of symbolic enforcement actions designed not only to get the agency on the map and give its employees a sense of purpose and pride, but also to warn polluting companies that the time would soon come for them to shoulder the burden of environmental cleanup. That accelerated the process of environmental cleanup beyond the real powers of the agency to make it happen.

Thus, the simple phrase "pollution abatement" defined a sustainable compact between society and the organization. It identified the direction in which public value lay. It forged a (more or less permanent, and more or less unanimous) political coalition. And it indicated what capabilities the EPA had to develop. As such, the phrase provided Ruckelshaus with both a mandate and a rough guide as to what actions he should take as a manager. In this sense, the phrase functioned as the cornerstone of a plan for the short- to medium-run future of the EPA. It obviously was not a "blueprint" for building and operating the organization. It was too general and thematic to be that. But that generality was a virtue because it allowed Ruckelshaus to be opportunistic and flexible in seizing possibilities as they came along. It became the touchstone against which all possible events or actions could be evaluated — those that happened to Ruckelshaus, as well as those he initiated. That is what makes the conclusions of strategic analysis so useful.

Strategic Concepts In Policing

To bring this idea closer to home, one can analyze the strategic properties of phrases that are often used to describe the mission of police departments — namely, professional law enforcement or professional crime fighting. This, too, can be analyzed as a proposed compact between police departments and the rest of society, and as something that guides the actions of police executives.

In substantive terms, the phrases embody a judgment that the most important purpose of the police is to enforce laws that protect life and property from criminal attack. The most visible emphasis is on enforcing the laws against murder, rape, robbery, burglary and assault — the crimes that are included as "Part I Crimes" in the Federal Bureau of Investigation's Uniform Crime Reports.

The phrase "professional law enforcement" could also refer to something far broader than this. It could, and often does, include enforcement of traffic laws and city health and safety ordinances. It could, and often does, include enforcement of the laws protecting citizens' rights not to be harassed by other citizens or the police themselves.

For the most part, however, society and the police understand these phrases to have the narrower meaning set out above. That is why the concept of "professional crime fighting" is, in many ways, a more accurate phrase than "professional law enforcement" in describing police purposes. "Professional law enforcement" is nonetheless preferred because it accommodates the wide range of

23

activities the police engage in while emphasizing the crime control aspects of those activities.

In political terms, these phrases are designed primarily to appeal to a constituency that is interested in controlling or reducing crime. That, of course, is what the police have mostly promised to do for society. It is a little less obvious but equally important that the phrase also promises to protect many important legal virtues such as impartiality, nonintrusiveness, and minimal use of force. That is an important part of the appeal of the word "professional." In the context of law enforcement, "professional" means not only technically competent, but also disciplined and fair in the way that laws are enforced. Indeed, it is the inclusion of this word that separates the modern era of policing from the bad old days of incompetence, corruption and brutality. It is also what separates modern public police departments from comparison and competition with the growing ranks of private security guards, whose "professionalism" is suspect, given loose entry standards, limited training and low wages.

In operational terms, the phrases direct one's attention to key factors that police administrators must manage. They make the power of the law—symbolized in badge, gun and uniform—the defining, distinctive competencies of police organizations. They make the enforcement of the law (in a fair and impartial way) the key task of the organization. They direct the attention of police managers to efforts to ensure that their officers are trained and equipped to perform this function. Thus, training tends to emphasize knowledge of the law and the disciplined use of force. Administrative arrangements are made to ensure that force, when deployed to make arrests, is properly used.

Given these characteristics, it is not surprising that these phrases are commonly used to describe the basic mission of police agencies. Like the concept of "pollution abatement," the concept of "professional law enforcement" defines a sustainable compact between the organization and the rest of society, and it directs managers' attention to the most important social values that must be protected or advanced in their organizations' operations. The question that is addressed in the remainder of this essay is whether these phrases represent the best strategic concept to guide the organization and management of police departments or whether more powerful concepts are now emerging. The techniques to be used in answering this question are the techniques of strategic analysis.

Chapter 2

Defining the Police Mission

A Strategic View of the Organizational Mission

If there is one thing that management studies have consistently shown, it is that there is no one best way to structure and manage an organization.[1] It all depends on the purposes of the organization, the environment in which the organization operates and the particular ways in which the organization might best be used to deal with particular problems. Consequently, before considering the best way to organize and manage a particular police department, one must define its mission.

In the traditional orthodoxy of police management, the job of the police department was to fully and faithfully enforce the laws. This mission statement, however, left unanswered the question of which laws were to be enforced, and by what methods. It also left unclear what specific changes citizens might expect as a result of the police department's efforts. And it left hanging the important question of whether and how the police might serve their communities through devices other than enforcing the law.

A strategic approach to defining an organizational mission takes a much different tack. As stated earlier, it does not assume that the goals or purposes of the organization are fixed and immutable; instead, it assumes that they are to be discovered by imaginative, value-seeking executives who are constantly searching for more effective, higher value uses of the assets entrusted to them by their communities. What such executives are looking for is a better "fit" between the problems, needs and desires of their communities and their organization's capabilities to respond. If there is a problem such as drugs, fear or economic decay for which their organization might be part or all of the solution, then they are eager to ensure that their organization makes the greatest possible contribution.

A corollary is that strategic-minded executives do not think of their organization's capabilities as fixed. Instead, they see their organizations as having distinctive competencies built through past investments and accumulated experience. While such competencies may have been created to serve particular, well-defined purposes (such as being able to respond quickly to crimes in progress), it often turns out that the same capabilities are valuable in other situations (such as stilling citizen fears or responding to medical or social emergencies). Consequently, it becomes a strategic question as to how an organization's current capabilities might best be used to deal with a community's current problems.

Moreover, organizational strategists know that their organization's capabilities may be altered over time through a process of challenge, investment and organizational support for the development of new capabilities. Consequently, if there is a need or an opportunity that now seems slightly beyond an organization's current grasp, that does not necessarily mean that the organization should not try to respond. It all depends on whether the new task seems sufficiently urgent and valuable to justify the risks of new investments and experimentation.

Finally, strategic managers evaluate the attractiveness of undertaking new tasks not only in terms of the urgency of the problems and the unique capacities of their organizations to respond, but also in terms of whether their efforts will be valued by their overseers in the authorizing environment. If the task is sufficiently urgent and important, if they are well positioned to respond and if the authorizing environment will value their efforts, then investments and experiments that would otherwise be foolhardy become prudent and valuable.

The point of these observations is simply this: that one can seek to define the mission of a police department by trying to discover the unchanging essence of policing, or by thinking through the question of how particular police departments, embodying particular kinds of competencies and capabilities, might make the greatest contributions to the quality of life in the communities in which they operate. We think that the latter is a better way of using valuable police resources, and it is in this spirit that we have sought to define the police mission.

The Central Importance of Crime Control

All discussions of the police mission begin with the subject of crime control. Indeed, to many, the discussions begin and end with this subject. To them, all else the police might do is not only secondary, but a dangerous and wasteful distraction from the primary business of the police. Crime control has this status for three reasons.

First, crime control is an urgent and compelling social task. And, it seems to have become more important over time. The hope that the police might succeed in reducing crime is what sustains public support for the police. The threat that crime might become uncontrollable if policing were neglected or changed is used as a club to ward off budget cuts or any other proposals to change the way police departments operate.

Second, the police (as they are currently constituted, organized and managed) seem particularly well suited to dealing with the problem of crime on behalf of society. Both society and the police think of criminal law, with its capacity to deter and incapacitate offenders, as an extremely powerful instrument in dealing with crime. The police are uniquely qualified to invoke that power.[2] They are organized to be on the lookout for crime, and to be immediately mobilizable by those who witness or are victimized by criminal offenses. They are specially trained to recognize when an arrest is appropriate or required, and to use force if necessary to ensure that citizens will submit to the orderly process of justice.

Third, crime control is the purpose that attracts the greatest enthusiasm and commitment from the police themselves. Many officers join police departments to become members of the "thin blue line" that protects decent people from predatory criminals. The aspects of their training that are psychologically most compelling emphasize the skills associated with bringing force to bear on angry, resistant citizens: driving fast, shooting a pistol and using come-along holds. The things that qualify them for assignment promotion to detective bureaus are most closely related to their ability to make arrests. As a result, a culture forms in the police department that sees crime fighting as not only the most important function, but the only honorable one.[3]

These powerful factors have, in the past, enshrined crime fighting as the dominant — even exclusive — purpose of a police department. Recently, however, other powerful forces have begun to undermine the notion that crimefighting is the only way to use the assets of a police department for the benefit of society. Ironically, the most powerful force leading police executives to rethink their exclusive preoccupation with crime control is their accumulating knowledge and sophistication about the nature of crime and the strengths and limitations of their current approaches to dealing with it.[4]

The Limitations of Reactive Approaches

The dominant characteristic of the current approach to policing is that it is "reactive." The police tend to wait until a crime occurs and an alarm is sounded before they respond. This reactive approach has some important advantages. It ensures that the police do not intrude too deeply into social life, and that when they do intrude, there is an important reason for it. In this sense, the reactive approach economizes on the use of the state's authority.

The police do not rely exclusively on reactive approaches, however. Patrol operations seek to deter crimes before they happen, as well as to ensure that a car is nearby if a serious crime occurs. Directed patrol operations increase the likelihood that crimes will be thwarted in progress.

Invisible Offenses

With respect to crimes such as narcotics offenses and extortion, the police have turned to more proactive efforts such as the recruitment of informants, the use of electronic surveillance and undercover operations to unearth offenses and prosecute the offenders.[5] The police have also used these methods to deal with street crimes such as robbery and burglary.[6] Still, it is largely true that the police response to crime is reactive, and that police executives sense the limits of that approach.

Police know the weaknesses of the reactive approach in dealing with crimes that do not produce victims or witnesses who mobilize the police and identify the offenders.[7] The reactive approach has never worked well with so-called "victimless" crimes, such as drug dealing, prostitution and gambling. Increasingly, however, the police are aware of these same limitations in dealing with robbery, burglary and other ordinary street offenses. These offenses should produce victims and witnesses willing to testify, but in today's cities, victims and witnesses frequently do not come forward because they are afraid to.[8] The reactive approach fails to reach extortion by youth gangs, casual violence within housing projects, rape within marriages and abuse and neglect of children for the same reason: no victim or witness reliably comes forward to report the offense.

Crime Prevention

Police executives are also frustrated by their apparent inability to prevent crimes. Rather than having to wait for a crime to occur before taking action, they would prefer to intervene before the crime occurs and protect citizens from the pain of criminal victimization.

The reactive approach to crime control does have some preventive effects on crime, of course. To the extent that the prospect of arrest, prosecution and punishment deters criminal offenders, the reactive approach to crime control (which creates precisely that threat) will prevent crimes.[9] To the extent that imprisonment prevents offenders from committing crimes while they are under state control, the successful arrest, prosecution and confinement of offenders prevents crimes.[10] To the extent that confinement subsequent to conviction can be used to persuade offenders that there are better ways to live their lives, as well as equip them with skills, the current approach to crime control may lay the basis for crime prevention.[11] In effect, the fact that the reactive approach allows one offense does not mean that it is ineffective in preventing future offenses by that offender.

Still, the charge that the police are not doing enough to prevent crime has some bite. No one expects the police to prevent crime by eliminating the root causes of crime. But there must be some approach that lies between alleviating all the ills of society on the one hand and lying in wait for an offender to commit a crime on the other.

In pursuit of crime prevention, the police have sometimes strayed into certain kinds of social work to which they seem particularly well suited. Many police departments, for example, have taken it on themselves to provide drug abuse resistance education.[12] Others have assigned officers to work with teenage gangs to avoid fights. But there are important methods of crime prevention that are much less like social work.

The frontier of policing now being explored is defined by the idea that some circumstances, or attributes of circumstances, might be "criminogenic," and that those circumstances could be eliminated with relatively little effort.[13] For example, a crowded street with cash-and-carry merchants jammed up against check-cashing storefronts might be a set of conditions that breed larcenies against persons. A dark hallway in a largely abandoned housing project might facilitate a rape that would otherwise not occur. A youth nightclub that closes after much of the public transportation has stopped running might create conditions leading to fights among the teenagers or fear and anger among the citizens living in adjacent neighborhoods.[14] Rent control policies that give landlords incentives to rent to new tenants may lead them to harass their current tenants, and the tenants to retaliate.[15]

As police departments are now organized, it would be hard to discover such conditions. The bulk of police resources are used to respond to and describe incidents, not the underlying problems or conditions that produce the incidents.[16] Yet increasingly, police departments are discovering that if they look behind the incidents, they can identify such problems.[17] And with further digging, they can understand what is causing the problem, and devise effective solutions.[18]

Police also are discovering that the solution does not necessarily lie in arrest.[19] Success often depends on other responses, such as mobilizing other city agencies to take remedial action, organizing private citizens to deal with an underlying problem or mediating a dispute without recourse to the courts. Indeed, police departments are learning that many of the calls they receive come from the same place, and that if they can deal with the underlying problem, they can not only prevent crimes that might emerge from the dangerous circumstances, but they can also reduce future calls for service.[20] This is a kind of crime prevention that is neither social work nor law enforcement.

Fear Reduction

A third frustration that police executives experience in pursuing their crime control mission comes from the discovery that citizens' fears are not necessarily closely tied to the objective facts of criminal victimization.[21] All police executives take for granted that their crime control mission includes the goal of reducing fear as well as reducing criminal victimization. They have also long assumed that the best (and only responsible) way to reduce fear is to successfully reduce criminal victimization. Consequently, the two distinct objectives have been seen as closely aligned. Recent empirical research has undermined these convenient assumptions, however. Citizens' fears are surprisingly uncorrelated with the real risks of criminal victimization.[22] Fear seems to be triggered more often by "incivilities," such as noisy teenagers, garbage on the streets, graffiti and a general atmosphere of decline and indifference, than by actual levels of crime. In this sense, fear is a problem separate and apart from criminal victimization.

It has also become clear that fear is a socially costly component of the overall crime problem.[23] It is causing citizens to buy an array of security devices, such as locks, guns and dogs, and to hire private security guards. Even worse, it is causing citizens to stay at home, regard their fellow citizens with suspicion, even change their residence. Paradoxically, while such efforts may make individual citizens feel more secure, they are making the broader society more dangerous, for they tear apart the social networks and informal mechanisms of social control that, in a healthy society, do most of the work of crime control and fear reduction.

These efforts are also undermining the commitment to public security by shifting the balance of security efforts toward private individuals and security firms. Yet, even with all these precautions, citizens still feel afraid. These trends signal an important shortcoming in the current approach to crime control and fear reduction.[24]

Research has shown that there are some things that police departments can do to reduce fear.[25] Probably the most important is to be as much of a presence in the minds of the citizens as possible. This means getting out of cars and talking to people. Apparently, in spite of the 911 systems with all their capabilities, people do not have a reassuring sense that the police are available. Only personal contacts sustained over time seem to produce that effect.

Taken together, these facts about fear pose an important strategic question for police executives, namely, whether fear should be acknowledged and responded to as a problem in its own right. The observations reported above make a compelling case for seeing fear as an important, separate problem. But there are lingering concerns that the resources devoted to dealing with fear might better be spent on reducing real criminal victimization. There is the sense that stilling fears in a world in which real criminal victimization has remained unchanged is a cynical and dangerous shell game. Whether the reasons against allocating police resources specifically to fear reduction are valid depends a great deal on whether the police can, in fact, reduce criminal victimization, and whether one can reasonably view citizens' fears as irrational. These are hard questions.

In sum, thoughtful police executives, taking crime control as their primary mission and rigorously pursuing the logic of this enterprise in light of their experience, are beginning to understand that crime will not necessarily yield to their current approaches. Their reactive strategy does not reach some important crimes. It does not give them broad enough opportunities to prevent crime. And it does not necessarily reach subjective fears of crime. In short, police executives are beginning to think that they should describe their mission in terms of crime prevention and fear reduction as well as crime control. In this, they are following a course that parallels developments in the field of medicine, where the focus on treating illness is gradually yielding to the importance of promoting wellness through increased attention to prevention and the elimination of "risk factors" that increase the likelihood of illness.[26]

Community Roles in Crime Control

A second major factor influencing current thought about the role of the police is the discovery of the extent to which the police are dependent on the community for their success in crime control efforts. This realization has emerged as the police have explored the efficacy of their current programmatic technologies in controlling crime.

The Weakness of Unilateral Police Action

Over the past few decades, the hardest blows that the field has had to absorb are those research results indicating that the principal programs on which the police were relying to control crime had only a limited effect. Through the Kansas City Patrol experiment, the field learned that varying levels of random patrol had little impact on levels of crime or fear.[27] Indeed, citizens did not even recognize when patrols had been increased or reduced in their areas.[28] Through additional studies in Kansas City and elsewhere, the field learned that rapid response to calls for service did not reduce crime and did not necessarily result in increased arrests.[29] Through a series of studies of the investigative process, the field learned that detectives were crucially dependent on the quality of information provided by victims and witnesses.[30] If they could identify the offender, the crime could be solved. If they could not, only rarely could forensic wizardry fill the gap.

These studies helped police understand how crime and fear could be increasing even as more resources were being devoted to policing. Many other factors contributed to the increasing crime rates—adverse social and economic trends, broad demographic trends increasing the absolute number of people in crime-prone age groups, and limited capacities to prosecute and punish those offenders the police caught. It became increasingly plausible, however, that weaknesses in the police strategy were also at least partly to blame. This was the bad news.

Citizen Contributions to Police Efficacy

The good news was that the studies pointed to improvements in the strategy of policing. Specifically, they reminded police executives of a crucial fact that they had forgotten as they sought to perfect the crime-fighting capabilities of their organizations, namely, that the police cannot succeed in their efforts to control crime and still fears without an effective partnership with the communities they police. Indeed, it became clear once again that the community itself was the first line of defense in controlling crime.

The fact that the police could not succeed without the active assistance of the community became apparent once one looked closely at how the police strategy really worked. Many offenses occurred in alleyways, hallways and kitchens—far from the view of patrolling police officers.[31] Without the eyes and ears of private citizens to extend the scope of police surveillance, the reach of police patrol was pathetically limited and superficial.

Similarly, unless citizens were willing to call the police, the rapid response capability that had been so carefully constructed was essentially useless.[32] And, if the call to the police came late, the police could not thwart the crime nor catch the offender. All they could do was comfort the victim and initiate an investigation.

Finally, unless citizens provided descriptions of offenders, police detectives were limited in their ability to solve crimes and mount an effective prosecution.[33] In this sense, the vigilance and motivation of citizens were integral parts of police operations. If that piece of the machinery was not working well, or was not reliably hooked up to the police, the expensive investments in police capabilities would be ineffective.

Self-Defense and Private Security

The fact that the communities were the first line of defense was driven home by an important, unexpected development. As fear of violence has increased, over the past decade, citizens have increasingly turned to private self-defense rather than public policing. Expenditures on private security have risen much more rapidly than expenditures on public police.[34] Employment in private security has also grown much faster than employment in public agencies.[35]

To discover that citizens would mobilize themselves in citizen block watches, that they would call in the Guardian Angels and the Black Muslims, that they would hire Burns Security Guards to allay their fears and control crime was a startling and sobering experience for police executives who had grown accustomed to thinking of themselves as society's only response to crime and fear. It reminded them that public police agencies were only a century or so old and that prior to that time policing had been done entirely by private citizens. The fact that they were implicitly (and sometimes explicitly) competing with private security activities for a share of the security business made them rethink their role and the way they wanted to relate to the communities they policed. And it suggested that if they could harness and guide, rather than ignore or compete with, private security efforts, the overall capacity of society to deal with crime and fear might be increased.

Building Effective Partnerships

If the police are operationally dependent on assistance from citizens and if citizens must inevitably be the first line of defense in controlling crime, then the question of what the police must do to mobilize and guide the citizenry becomes crucially important. The past answer of the police has been to be responsive to the citizenry by answering individual calls for service quickly. That has not, however, created effective working partnerships between citizens and the police. There seem to be two reasons for this.

First, it is by no means clear that the police response to the incidents has been very satisfactory. The citizens called the police because they wanted help. The police arrived on the scene with a strong sense that they were only interested in serious crimes and that the only question that needed addressing was whether someone had broken a law. If the incident did not involve a crime, or if no arrest seemed appropriate, the police were eager to cut short the encounter with the citizen and get back "in-service." Such responses did not necessarily make many friends among citizens, nor increase their enthusiasm for calling the police the next time.

Second, responding to incidents phoned in by individual citizens produced police responses at the wrong level of aggregation. As noted above, it focused police attention on incidents rather than the larger and more lasting underlying problems. It made the police think of their clients as individuals rather than groups. Both things have made it hard for the police to form partnerships with existing community groups or to help form ones in places where they do not exist. Such activities have also been inhibited by the organizational structure of police departments. The functional organization of departments implies that geographically based community groups cannot gain convenient access to them. There is no one in a department who shares their particular geographical perspective.

The question thus becomes to what extent the police are prepared to adapt their operations, style and structure to strengthen their relations with community networks. The reason they might wish to do so is that it would strengthen their capacity to control crime by slightly deflecting their current preoccupation with crime enough to make the concerns that citizens bring them worth greater attention. The basic idea is that one spends time building the relationship so the relationship is strong when it is tested in dealing with crime. To try to deal with crime without developing that relationship is fruitless. Yet, one cannot build the relationship by concentrating exclusively on crime.

These observations are causing police executives to rethink the role of the community in crime control efforts and consider how the relationship might best be developed.

Other Uses of the Police

The last important factor shaping police views about their mission is the simple fact that citizens want to use them for many purposes other than crime control. This fact emerges plainly from any analysis of calls for service or of what police do when they are on patrol.[36] The simple reality is that crime fighting in the form of interrupting crimes in progress or pursuing fleeing offenders occupies far less than 10% of the time of a patrol force.[37] The bulk of the time is taken up with other matters, such as giving information to citizens, filling out reports, responding to medical emergencies and mediating conflicts among citizens that have not yet escalated into crimes.

It is also fairly clear that when the police talk to communities through meetings with concerned citizens (rather than over the 911 system), the citizens are rarely concerned with what the police regard as serious crimes. They are far more interested in discussing matters the police would consider minor such as disorderly bars, inadequate garbage collection, poor street lighting and the like.[38] In short, citizens want to use the police force for many purposes other than reducing robbery and burglary.

It is no accident that citizens routinely use the police for these other purposes. It reflects the fact that citizens in today's cities have many needs and fears and that the police have many capabilities that are useful to citizens beyond their ability to fight crime. Although the police may think of themselves as a crime-fighting force, the citizens see a large corps of trained and resourceful public employees, available to them around the clock for the price of a phone call. They also correctly see that the police officer's formal authority can be quite helpful to them in mediating a variety of disputes, even when those disputes have not ripened into crimes or civil court cases. They also know that the stature and prestige of the officers might be helpful to them as they seek to organize their own neighborhood activities or seek assistance from other governmental agencies.

The police have a wider and more useful set of operational capabilities than they like to acknowledge. Or, put somewhat differently, the capabilities that the police have created to help them fight crime turn out to have value to the citizenry for other purposes. Citizens are not shy about claiming this value in the alternative uses.

The important question facing police executives is whether these noncrime-related claims on police departments represent an abuse of the police by citizens or an indication of different ways of using police departments to contribute to the quality of community life. Private sector executives who learned that people were using their products for some purpose other than what was originally intended would regard that as good news. They would begin orienting their companies to produce what citizens really wanted. In the same view, public libraries have recently discovered that they were being used as after school child-care centers by working parents. While most librarians viewed such activities as an abuse of the libraries, others looked at the situation and wondered whether it would be valuable to add that function to the library's traditional functions. It seemed to them that it was something the citizens wanted and needed. It also provided an opportunity to promote reading.

No doubt, these perspectives go too far for police executives. It is their duty, after all, to preserve a crime-fighting capability so that the citizens can have it when they need it, just as it is the librarians' duty to preserve a book collection for public use. Public executives cannot simply pander to every individual citizen's desire to use public institutions to advance their special purposes. But citizens' demands do help to pose sharply the question of to what extent police departments should accommodate these demands.

Police executives can respond to the question in three ways. First, they can decide that these demands are dangerous distractions from their essential focus and do what they can to wall off the demands or shift them to other agencies. Second, they can decide that responding to these demands is consistent with their basic crime-fighting mission and, therefore, important to accommodate. Providing services to needy citizens, responding to social and medical emergencies and mediating disputes as they occur advance crime-fighting objectives in two ways. On one hand, they sometimes help to prevent crimes by eliminating some of the conditions that lead to crimes. On the other, they build a relationship of confidence with the community that is a necessary part of effective attacks on serious crime. Third, police executives can decide that these noncrime-related activities are worth doing in their own right and that the police are uniquely positioned to perform these services as well as to fight crime. In the interest of making the maximum possible contribution to the communities they serve, they will yield to the inevitable and become skilled in supplying the services that the citizens inevitably demand from them.

Obviously, which decision a police executive makes has crucial implications for the definition of the police function and for the enthusiasm that citizens feel for their police department. The decision also has important implications for the kinds of capabilities that must be developed within the department.

Summary: The Business of Policing

As one thinks about policing today's cities, it becomes more and more difficult to think only in terms of crime control accomplished through patrol, rapid response to calls for service and retrospective investigation. The reason is not so much that the urgency surrounding crime control has diminished. Indeed, if anything, it has increased. Nor is it because current police capabilities have no value in crime control. Quite the contrary. The dominant place in policing will always be reserved for patrol operations designed to deter and thwart crimes and for investigations designed to identify and build strong cases against criminal offenders.

Police executives must look beyond pure crime control and see whether they can devise a more effective strategy for policing America's cities by taking advantage of their increasingly sophisticated understanding of crime. Specifically, we must figure out how we can help prevent crimes by learning how to identify and resolve the more underlying causes of crime. We must also determine whether fear is a separate problem worth addressing and how it might best be managed.

It is also important to acknowledge the crucial role of individual citizens and community groups in dealing with crime. Ways must also be found to channel self-defense activities into a partnership with public police forces rather than have them dissipate in the continued growth of individualistic private security efforts. And finally, it is important to decide whether police departments should accommodate the demands now being made on them to provide noncrime-related services, and to open themselves to discussions with communities about the department's priorities.

The right answers and the right decisions to be made about these matters are by no means clear. The force of the arguments against taking too narrow a view of the police function is growing, however. In pursuit of crime control, and as a result of the capabilities they have developed in seeking to control crime, they are being drawn into a far broader and more intimate engagement with community life than originally envisioned by contemporary police theorists.

It seems that there is societal value in fully acknowledging, not only in operations but also in philosophy, the wide set of police functions identlfied by Herman Goldstein 13 years ago:[39]

- To prevent and control conduct widely recognized as threatening to life and property (serious crime).

- To aid individuals who are in danger of physical harm, such as the victim of a criminal attack.

- To protect constitutional guarantees, such as the right of free speech and assembly.

- To facilitate the movement of people and vehicles.

- To assist those who cannot care for themselves: the intoxicated, the addicted, the mentally ill, the physically disabled, the old, and the young.

- To resolve conflict, whether it be between individuals, groups of individuals, or individuals and their government.

- To identify problems that have the potential for becoming more serious problems for the individual citizen, for the police, or for the government.

- To create and maintain a feeling of security in the community.

In short, it seems that police departments might do better in terms of crime control, ensuring organizational growth and success, and helping the nation's cities deal with their problems if they widened their conception of their proper functions, diversified their approaches to performing the varied functions and organized themselves to develop strong partnerships with the communities they serve. If true, this conclusion has very important implications for how the police should be constituted, organized and managed. It also means that leadership will be required to move the police from their current position to the desired future position.

Chapter 3

Constituting Police Departments

Strategy and Political Management

For most police executives, the necessity of participating in the external, political environment is a painful and distasteful part of their job. As they encounter mayors, city council members, civil service commissions and the media in the course of their regular duties, they feel both vulnerable and corruptible: vulnerable because their jobs, reputations and careers are to some degree hostage to the views that such people have of their performance, and corruptible not only because they might be asked to do something that goes against their own best professional judgment, but also because they might be tempted by the allure of celebrity status to spend more time in the limelight than they (or their organization) think they should. Thus, many police executives seek to minimize the political aspects of their jobs.

Viewed from a strategic perspective, however, this is a great mistake. The strategic perspective reminds police executives that they are dependent on continuing credibility with their overseers to ensure a continuing supply of resources to their organizations. Without substantial credibility, their freedom to maneuver—to develop and build their organizations—is quite limited. Even more importantly, police executives need a great deal of operational assistance from private citizens, community groups and other agencies of government to perform their tasks well. And, from an ethical perspective, police executives must be accountable to their authorizing environments for their performance and that of the departments they lead. Thus, for both practical and ethical reasons, police executives must engage their political environments regularly and often.

A corollary of this observation is that skillful management of the authorizing environment can yield enormous dividends in terms of improved operational performance. This is most obvious when departments enjoy a high degree of credibility within their communities, and can therefore command substantial resources and authority to be used in the performance of their duties. It is a lucky department that is in that position.

When a department is not in that position, however, it is up to the executive to find some way of enhancing the credibility of the department. One route that many executives have followed in the past is that of enhanced professionalism. In the hopes that they could increase the prestige and standing of the department in the eyes of the community many police executives have raised entry standards, increased training for officers, instituted more effective controls over the conduct of officers and developed more sophisticated technical capabilities. Although changes such as these have sometimes resulted in greater resources and greater professional autonomy for the department, many executives have learned the painful lesson that professionalism and autonomy do not always lead to increased support and legitimacy for the department.

Some executives have pursued increased support and legitimacy by becoming more responsive to community aspirations and demands. This approach seems to work reliably in terms of cultivating political support, but executives and officers alike often feel that such "pandering" to community demands threatens the professionalism and autonomy of the organization. And it is clear that there are many demands that the community would like to make on a police department that a professional department would be duty bound to reject: for example, a demand that the police run all suspected drug dealers out of a park, or that it deploy a substantial portion of its resources in the richest areas of a community or that it respond to political pressures in promoting or assigning officers to key positions. Still, increased responsiveness to community concerns beckons as an often successful approach to increasing the support and legitimacy of a department.

Thus, the challenge in the political management of police departments is to find a proper balance between professionalism and autonomy on the one hand, and accountability and responsiveness on the other. How to strike this balance is the focus of Chapter 3.

Fiduciary Responsibilities of Police Executives

Police departments, and the executives who lead them, are entrusted with important public resources.[1] The most obvious are tax dollars, taken from private use by force of law. An even more precious resource is the authority to bring the power of the state to bear on individual citizens suspected of wrongdoing. That resource, too, is surrendered to the police by private citizens. It comes not from their pocketbook, but from their precious stock of liberty.

In a democracy, and particularly one that loves private enterprise and liberty as much as ours does, both tax dollars and public authority are in short supply. They are supplied to public enterprises only with great reluctance, and their use is closely monitored by citizens and their representatives. Citizens expect and demand that the public monies granted to the police will be used efficiently and fairly to produce public security. They assume the same about the use of public authority.

To ensure a continuing flow of resources to police departments, then, the police must be able to explain how those resources will be used to make life better for the community as a whole. That explanation is contained in the description the police give of their basic mission and purposes. If the explanation is accepted by those who authorize police operations, it becomes the mandate for policing—the basis on which policing is founded. Statements about broad purposes alone, however, are not sufficient to maintain a flow of resources to the police. To maintain their credibility and enhance their autonomy, the police must achieve what they promise to achieve, and produce what they promise to produce. It is the record of accomplishment contained in reports filed with different kinds of overseers and authorizers that maintains police credibility in the community.

The Current Mandate

The current strategy of policing—described as professional law enforcement—seeks to establish legitimacy and continuing support on three strong pillars. The first is the enduring popularity of crime control. Insofar as crime remains an urgent concern of citizens, and the police are seen as the best response to citizens' fears, the police will enjoy enthusiastic support.

The second is the claim to impartiality and technical competence in law enforcement that is implicit in the concept of professionalism. It is this claim that seeks to assure worried citizens that the money and authority entrusted to the police will be used economically and fairly. It will not be spent recklessly to indulge police aspirations.

The third is the commitment to serve individual citizens symbolized by a patrol force organized to respond instantly to calls for assistance. This is the most concrete and direct promise the police now make. The other commitments are abstract and build only abstract support. Getting to the citizens when they call is concrete and immediate. It is in these transactions that the public image of policing is forged.

Political Accountability and Police Independence

One of the important features of this particular vision of policing is that it makes a virtue of police independence from political interference. Because society has learned to value the impartial administration of justice and the ideal of a professionally competent police department, the police have been insulated from some forms of political interference. Chiefs of police are often protected from arbitrary firing by special civil rules.[2] Appointments to and promotions within police departments are strictly regulated by civil service rules.[3] Police departments have fought to develop and hold to technical bases, rather than political power, for assigning patrol forces.[4] Mayors have been reluctant to intervene publicly in police affairs lest they be accused of political interference.[5]

The acknowledged importance of maintaining police independence from political interference has misled some police executives (and even more police officers) to imagine that the police are wholly autonomous and that any kind of political oversight is improper. In their view, they should be allowed to enforce the law in the ways that they see fit. Elected chief executives of local governments and neighborhood associations should keep their noses out of police department operations.

The reality is that the police, like all public institutions, must remain accountable both to citizens (through their elected representatives) and to the law. They are broadly accountable to the chief executive of the local government for which they work. They are accountable to the special oversight agencies, such as the civil service commission and budget agencies, that monitor their use of money and people. They are accountable to citizens through media coverage of their activities. And they remain accountable to the courts, not only through the courts' responses to the cases they bring against criminal defendants but also through the civil suits filed by citizens against the police for improper conduct.[6]

Police accountability to these agencies is morally and legally required. It is also practically necessary. However much the police like to complain about the irrationality, unreliability and impropriety of oversight from these agencies, the practical reality is that any of these agencies can rise up in indignation at the police and force them to change their operations. A mayor can convene a commission to review the police use of deadly force, and the conclusions of that commission can be made binding on the police.[7] A civil service commission can reject a police plan for upgrading the professional qualifications of its officers, or a budget bureau can claim that police methods for allocating officers are flawed.[8] A newspaper story about a sloppy drug investigation or a pedestrian fatality in a high-speed auto chase can trigger a review of the department's policies in those domains. A citizen, abused by the police during an arrest, can file a civil complaint against the officer and the department as a whole. Such actions will have important consequences for police policies and operations.

Current Terms of Accountability

What the police have done to protect their autonomy and limit outside intrusions is to seek to narrow, and establish their own, terms of accountability. The concepts of "professional law enforcement" and "effective crime fighting" implicitly define dimensions of accountability. To a degree, their commitment to these concepts makes the police vulnerable to criticism. By embracing the goal of crime control, the police have made themselves at least partly responsible for levels of crime in society. By committing themselves to professionalism, they have become accountable for the qualifications of their officers, the training they provide and the skill officers display in the field. By offering a broad service to the public, they invite individual citizens to make claims on them, and they make themselves accountable for the rapidity and comprehensiveness of their responses to calls for service.

These terms of accountability also offer protection to police departments. To the extent that the police perform well in these domains, their credibility, autonomy and legitimacy are increased. They might even be able to use successful performance in these domains as protection against criticism and intrusions when an inevitable mistake occurs.

In evaluating the current strategy of policing in terms of its ability to command public support and establish a coherent mandate for the police, it is important to note an unresolved tension at the core. The central issue is whether society cares more about "professional law enforcement" or more about "crime fighting."

When citizens consider the police "crime fighters," they think in terms of the results rather than the means. They applaud the toughness and courage that police bring to their jobs. They admire the technical skills that are employed to capture ruthless and dangerous offenders. They are impatient with legal rulings that "handcuff" the police. They like to see the bad guys behind bars. They regard civilian suits against the police as not the product of police misconduct, but of the avarice of money-hungry citizens and lawyers. This perspective dominates the public view of policing. It is even more common in the police view of policing.

Other times, however, citizens do not see the police this way. When the police accidentally shoot an unarmed teenager, break into a person's house without a warrant or are revealed to be taking bribes or extorting payoffs from drug dealers, then citizens suddenly see the police in a different light. At such moments, the police themselves appear to be criminals. Instead of glorying in police capacities to lock up bad guys, the citizens see the police as reckless or self-indulgent in the use of the power that was entrusted to them. They demand an accounting.

To a degree, citizens are justified in being indignant. Part of the ideal of police professionalism is that the police will use their powers in a disciplined and economical way. As noted above, that has been part of the promise the police have made to society over the past 30 years. It has also been one of the bases on which the police have sought and gained a degree of autonomy from close political oversight.

From the police perspective, however, the public indignation inevitably feels like a betrayal. After all, up until the event that triggered the public indignation, the police felt they were being encouraged to be tough. They experience the sudden onslaught of criticism as a shift in the political winds. At their worst moments, they see a conspiracy in such shifts: the sudden reemergence of a powerful but unrepresentative group of citizens—the liberals, the do-gooders, the academic lawyers, the civil libertarians, the "criminals' lobby."

The police are probably justified in feeling betrayed. The cycles of broad public support for the police as crime fighters followed by public indignation over police corruption and brutality seem to stem only partly from police performance. The cycles also come about because the public itself is quite ambivalent about its expectations of the police. The concern about police professionalism and discipline has been only imperfectly integrated in the public conception of the police mission. Society often winks at violations of the rules when the police are being effective in controlling crime. The laws regulating police conduct are seen as constraints rather than goals in themselves.

The public's ambivalence is clearly revealed in a survey of citizens' attitudes toward the Philadelphia Police

Department following the MOVE operation, in which police bombs ignited a fire that destroyed a city block and a federal investigation revealed extensive corruption in high levels of the department. In these circumstances, one might have thought that the citizens would be indignant about the police actions. In fact, they rated the Philadelphia Police Department's performance relatively high—70% rated the agency as good or excellent. Only 30% said they were doing a poor job.[9]

Philadelphia's citizens were also asked about specific forms of police misconduct. Fifty percent reported that the police were often rude.[10] Forty-nine percent thought the police took bribes sometimes or often.[11] What is surprising about these results is that the citizens gave the police high marks for overall effectiveness, even though they thought the police behaved quite badly in daily operations.

One obvious way to interpret these results is that the citizens thought the police were doing a good job of crime fighting and responding to calls for service, and on that basis they gave the department a high overall score. They also seemed to think that in order for the police to do these jobs well, they had to be indulged a little. They had to be allowed to sleep on the job, to be rude, to harass defendants, and to extort bribes.

This deal—effectiveness for indulgence—can be, and often is, made in many American cities. The deal is usually implicit, not explicit. It is talked about in locker rooms rather than in public forums. But it is there, lurking in the background. Its influence is what leads the police to cut corners in their crime control operations. Moreover, to many citizens and police officers it seems like the right deal to make. The deal accurately reflects and expresses their values. That view endures among the police until they finally recognize that the deal is unstable and unreliable. The values that are sacrificed in this deal—the values of fairness and economy in the use of public authority—are core values. When evidence becomes available that the police are sacrificing these values, there will be a backlash. In the backlash, police officers will be scapegoated, careers will be sacrificed and department morale will collapse.

The alternative to going through these up-and-down cycles is for the police and the public to work harder at integrating the competing values of effectiveness in crime fighting and disciplined use of public authority. This should not be so difficult. After all, among the laws that are the most important to enforce are those regulating the police. A professional law enforcement agency, as distinct from a crimefighting agency, would accept this as an important goal, not just as a troubling constraint. It would work to remind the public of their interest in a disciplined police force, even—perhaps especially—at those times when the citizens wished to grant the police wider formal and informal powers to garner greater effectiveness in crime control. In short, the police should stand for the values of fair and impartial law enforcement rather than ruthless crime fighting and vengeance.

The Current Structure of Accountability

Being clear about the values that the police should stand for in society is the key first step in establishing a secure and legitimate base for the police. The second step is being clear about the exact mechanisms of reporting to those to whom the police are accountable. Partly because the police have sought to insulate themselves from political interference, the current relations with authorizing bodies are fragile, inconstant and episodic.

To Whom Are the Police Accountable?

Police chiefs frequently do not have a direct reporting relationship to their elected or appointed executives. Instead, the police are linked to the political authority largely through budget submissions and annual reports. The principal statistical measures used in these reports to communicate their needs and accomplishments are statistics on crime rates, clearance rates and response times.

The police are accountable directly to the public through media coverage of their activities. This kind of exposure tends to focus principally on their performance in solving notorious cases or in dealing with instances of officer misconduct. Rarely do the media focus on broader issues of police performance, such as their allocation of resources, the organization of their dispatching operation and so on.

In an important sense, police are accountable to the citizens who call them for assistance. The speed of their response to these calls is one of the key statistics (however inappropriate) used in measuring police performance.[12] What the police do at the scene of the call is influenced significantly by the citizen's desires and his or her willingness to file charges.[13] And the concrete experience of the citizen's encounter with the police is one important basis on which the public view of the police force is formed.

Finally, police are accountable to the courts and other elements of the criminal justice system. Prosecutors and judges can choose to process police cases or reject them as inadequate. They can comment to the media and to professional associations about police performance. Judges may also be involved in holding the police accountable through civil liability.

Limitations of the Current System

A review of the current structure of accountability reveals two important characteristics. First, it focuses either on very broad, overall patterns of police conduct or on very specific incidents. The budgets, annual reports and professional gossip about the police all focus on the aggregate, overall performance of the department. The media stories and the civil suits focus on individual incidents, which may be seen as indicative of broader features of police performance. Indeed, it is partly what these incidents suggest about the police department's values and capabilities as a whole that makes them interesting and newsworthy. But the essential focus is on the individual incident. Rarely do individual incidents produce a serious analysis of aggregate performance.

The second characteristic is that the most powerful pressures on the police are those associated with the individual incidents. The pressures on the police to perform well on average and across the board are, in general, quite weak. Political authority does not demand this. The budget oversight imposes some financial discipline, but it does not demand productivity gains or innovations in policing. Indeed, the budget process often creates obstacles to innovation since it denies police executives the needed flexibility, and is intolerant of experimentation. The citizens' demands for overall improvements in policing are also quite weak. As a result, most departments are organized to avoid individual mistakes and to handle incidents well rather than to sustain broad improvements or initiate experiments in new ways of policing.

Some Alternatives

One can imagine some alternative mechanisms of accountability that would give citizens and community groups more of a voice. Civilian review boards are occasionally proposed as mechanisms for improving police accountability. They are handicapped, however, by their narrow focus on incidents of police misconduct and the resulting police hostility toward these boards.[14]

Some communities have created police commissions. Some are temporary, others are permanent. Some are established by law, others by more informal means. Some exist for limited purposes, such as appointing a chief; others have broader, more continuing powers and responsibilities. Depending on their responsibilities, the stature of their members, their history and their specific powers, the commissions can have more or less influence over police operations. In New South Wales, Australia, for example, a police board made up of the police commissioner and two influential citizens has the power to approve strategic plans submitted by the police department and to appoint top-level officials. The board has also provided the energy and the leverage necessary to produce important changes in the 9,000-person New South Wales Police Department.[15]

The most important innovation that seems to be occurring in structuring police accountability is the creation of community consultative groups.[16] Sometimes the police create these groups. Other times they explicitly "recognize" existing groups by meeting with them regularly. The significant fact about these groups is that they operate at a level of aggregation between the city as a whole and the individual citizen. Consequently, they see and are concerned about different problems than are seen at the two other levels. These groups also bring different capacities for actions supporting the police than are available at citywide or individual levels. They can influence decisions on how the police will behave and what standards they want enforced in their areas in a way that is impossible for the city as a whole to do.

The Paradox of External Accountability and Leadership

The principal worries in encouraging police responsiveness to the concerns of neighborhood consultative groups are that the police will lose some of their autonomy. Further, there is the worry that the police will become subject to the interests and needs of some elements of the community at the expense of others. Particularly worrisome is the possibility that the rich and well-organized communities will be able to demand more service from the police than the poor and disorganized ones.[17]

These potential pitfalls can be avoided if the police department keeps in mind the central values that it has pledged to maintain. Police executives are responsible for the professional development and integrity of their organization. They cannot yield to local groups their responsibilities for deploying the people and other resources entrusted to them. They are obligated to respond fairly to need rather than to political clout or ability to pay.

And they are obligated to protect the rights of minorities as well as those of the majority.

Strong mechanisms of external accountability are a key to legitimacy. Unless police organizations work hard to cultivate a constituency by expressing a commitment to important values and demonstrating that they can operate consistently with those values, there will be no one to support them when they are threatened.

Strong external accountability is also an important instrument of police leadership. This strikes many as a paradox. In their view, the strength of police leaders is measured by their independence and their ability to protect their spheres of professional competence. A strong police executive is one whose legitimacy is founded on his or her individual expertise and vision. That view is the legacy of Progressive Era reforms that sought to improve police management by separating police administration from politics and placing the responsibility for management in the hands of professionally competent executives. The reality, however, is that when the police were separated from politics, police leaders were not made independent. They simply became more dependent on the last remaining group that was interested in and capable of influencing police operations, namely, the police officers themselves. Without external accountability, the leverage police executives have over their own organizations is limited.

Thus, one of the important ways that police leaders can bolster their leadership and find an effective basis for challenging their own organizations is to create and animate their accountability to the broader public.[18] That is one of the important lessons that has been learned by those who first sought to professionalize the police and eliminate corruption and who are now trying to steer the police toward a strategy of community policing. Without public demands for less corruption or improved policing, stimulated through external accountability, police executives have limited power to lead.

Chapter 4

Managing Police Performance: Internal Organization and Control

Strategic Uses of Administrative Systems

Devising a successful strategy for a police department is critically dependent on defining the proper mission and goals and establishing proper external relations with the political environment. Ultimately, however, whether a strategy succeeds or not depends on whether the organization can be coaxed to perform as envisioned in the strategy.

The principal instruments a police executive uses to influence the overall performance of the organization are the familiar tools of administration—the organization of the department, the recruitment and development of the organization's personnel, the establishment of administrative controls over finances and operations and so on.

In thinking about how these instruments can be used to improve the performance of police organizations, police managers often assume that they may be relatively easily manipulated. They also often assume that there are general, technical answers to the question of how best to organize, staff and control a police department. Even worse, they assume that good management consists of importing the most advanced or sophisticated administrative systems into their organizations. As such managers seek to wield the instruments of administrative influence, however, they learn two painful lessons.

First, they discover that the instruments are quite difficult to manipulate. Reorganizations, for example, cannot be done at the whim of the chief executive.[1] Powerful interests inside and outside the department have stakes in the current structure of the organization. Personal status, opportunities for advancement, the nature of one's work and access to other people inside and outside the organization are all rooted in organizational structure. When a change is proposed, those interests are affected. If many are opposed to the change, the police executive may be powerless to effect it, even though he or she is ostensibly in charge. If many people other than the police executive have their hands on the administrative instruments (for example, civil service commissions, or budget and finance offices), then the executive can only earn the right to wield them through a complex political process that either persuades these others to agree to the necessary changes, or forces the others to relinquish enough control to move in the direction that the police executive desires.[2] The implication, then, is that these systems may be changed only slowly.

Second, administrative systems take a long time to produce their effects inside an organization, and they have somewhat unpredictable consequences. If a police executive redefines a manager's job through a reorganization, it takes a while for that manager to learn the content of the new job and how to perform it. Indeed, for a reasonably long time, the incumbent in the job may well resist the redefinition and continue operating on the basis of past understandings. If the executive grows frustrated and replaces the incumbent, it will take time for the new appointee to develop the working relations with his or her peers and subordinates that will enable the appointee to be effective in the job even if he or she understands it well. Similarly, a new accounting system may not produce any important changes in an organization's knowledge of its average costs, or in the incentives facing subordinate managers whose performance is being assessed in terms of the new system, until the system has been operating long enough to produce historical information that can be used for comparisons. That is often a period of several years.

Still, for all their limitations, these systems are ultimately what give the executive leverage over current operations. Changes that the executive desires cannot be said to have been accomplished until they are reflected in the organization's administrative systems. Indeed, that is often what is meant when one speaks of "institutionalizing" change. Manipulations of these systems are also often important in initiating and giving direction to a process of change as well as in consolidating desired changes.

Strategic managers take a much different view of how to use these administrative systems. They understand it is extremely time consuming to change the systems; consequently, if the effort is to be undertaken, it must be worth it in terms of improved performance or a stronger strategic position. Moreover, strategic managers judge the value of changes in the systems not in terms of whether they approach some technical ideal, but instead whether the changes will help to advance the overall strategy of the organization. In this view, decisions about structure, personnel and control must be made to serve the strategy that emerges from broader considerations of legitimacy and purpose and organizational capability. All too often, police managers tinker with organizational structure and personnel systems without being able to relate those decisions to the overall strategy of the organization. Yet being able to make that connection, and to see that it is the process of changing administrative systems incrementally over time that breathes practical life into strategic visions, is precisely what strategic management is all about.

For these reasons, managers must view the changes that they make in their organizations' administrative systems as strategic moves. They are strategic not only in the sense that they must support the overall strategy of the organization, but also in the sense that manipulations of the systems must be used incrementally to change the direction and style of the organization. They must be grasped opportunistically and must be held in place long enough to produce effects.

An important implication is that the particular administrative systems that would be appropriate for a department trying to go in a particular direction cannot be chosen in the abstract. They must be selected to suit the particular contexts in which they are to be used. In this important sense, there is probably no single "best way" to organize and manage a department.

Still, there are some things that can be said about the organization and management of police departments. There are some particularly important things to be said about internal administration if police executives decide to pursue a strategy of policing that seeks to deal more broadly with the problems facing the nation's cities and to take advantage of what has been learned about the substantive and administrative limits of the "reform strategy."

Organizing

Organizing concerns the definition of a structure of roles and reporting relationships within an organization.[3] The structure is not an end in itself, but a means to an end.[4] It must fit the task of the organization and the limitations of available resources and personnel.

Different Organizing Principles

Generally speaking, organizations can divide their work in three ways.[5] The most common is to divide the work by function. In a manufacturing enterprise, for example, a functional organization typically establishes departments of engineering, production, sales and finance as the primary units of the enterprise. A functionally organized police department would have an administrative services division, a patrol division and a detective or investigative division.

The second way to organize the work is on the basis of products or programs. A manufacturing company, for example, might organize itself into units that make different kinds of products: a soap division, a wax division and a brush division. A police department might organize itself into units that deal with different kinds of crime problems: a juvenile division, a drug division, a robbery division and a sex crimes division.

A third kind of organizational structure is one based on geographical areas. A manufacturing company organized with a northeast division, a southwest division and a Great Lakes division would follow a geographic logic. A police department with a Main Street division, a Lakeside division and a Hilldale division would be based on a similar logic.

Most organizations are hybrids in the sense that they have structural units based on all three concepts. Consequently, when one characterizes a given organization as functional, programmatic or geographic, one is usually describing the dominant logic in the organization, or the logic that is used to divide the organization at the highest level. In this sense, most police departments are functional organizations. The divisions made at the top of the organization typically divide the department into different functions rather than into different programmatic or geographical units. Still, most police departments have units defined in nonfunctional terms as well. Special units are often created to deal with particular kinds of crimes, such as juvenile delinquency or drugs. And, generally speaking, the patrol unit is subdivided into geographic units. The investigative unit may also be subdivided into units dealing with particular kinds of crime or with geographic responsibilities if the organization is large enough to sustain these specializations.

The functional structure of police departments has some important strengths. Most significant, it enables people to develop expertise in their functional domains. As important, it prevents special interest groups organized around specific geographic areas or specific kinds of crimes from exercising undue influence over police department operations, since there is no specially defined unit committed to dealing with their interests. Indeed, the decision to shift from a geographic structure of precinct commands to a functional structure was an important device in breaking the power of political machines organized on a geographic basis.

The functional structure also has some important weaknesses. It tends to promote parochialism and conflict within the organization as each function tries to claim the mantle of the most important function within the organization. It makes coordination across functional lines slow and difficult. It encourages managers to think of themselves as experts in their functions whose task it is to make sure that everyone under their command does the job right rather than as people whose special skills lie in getting others to work together. Most important, it means that the organization frustrates and fails to garner the support of neighborhood groups who find that there is no one short of the chief of police who can deal with their particular problem if it requires a multifunctional response.

Line, Staff and Support Units

Designing a suitable organizational structure for a police department also requires the police executive to understand the distinction among line, staff and support functions. Line functions are those that work directly on achieving the organization's objectives. In a police department, the patrol division, the detective bureau and the traffic division are all line functions. Staff functions are those that support top management's efforts to direct and guide the organization and to account for the organization's activities. In a police department, the budget unit, the planning and evaluation unit and the legal counsel's office are all staff units. Support functions are those activities that provide services to the rest of the organization and that cut across functional, programmatic or geographic lines.[6] Examples include personnel, vehicle maintenance and procurement activities.

A frequent problem with police organizations is that support or staff functions are placed within a single line unit. For example, it is not unusual to find the records section reporting to the commander of investigations. This may make sense if the investigators are the primary contributors and users of information from the records section. But it also means that the patrol bureau will find it difficult to gain access to the information and will be reluctant to contribute to it. If one hoped to get the patrol unit to produce better information for the records section, to conduct preliminary investigations or to use the records to plan directed patrol strategies, those aims would be frustrated by having the records section in the investigative unit rather than as a separate support unit serving all the organization's line operations.

Centralization and Decentralization

An additional organizational issue that must be resolved in organizing a police department concerns the number of levels in the organization and the degree of decentralization that is desirable. In the past, police organizations have been organized like military organizations with unified command authority, strict hierarchies and narrow spans of control. The aims of such organizational structures are essentially two. The first is to ensure effective discipline and control by providing for very close supervision and by pinpointing accountability for command decisions. The second is to enable the police force to form into units of varying size to deal with problems of varying size. While the standard operating unit of a police department is an individual officer on patrol or engaged in an investigation, it is sometimes necessary for the police department to form larger operational units to deal with special problems such as preventing a suspect from fleeing the scene of a crime, mounting an intensive investigation or manhunt and dealing with the visit of a celebrity or an outbreak of civil disorder. To ensure that these operations are coordinated, there must

74

be a rank structure that enables officers to assume command of operations of varying size.

The commitment to unified command, strict hierarchy and narrow spans of control has two important implications for the personnel systems of police departments. First, it tends to create very steep, vertical organizations with many different levels of middle management. Second, it tends to create career paths that make rising through the ranks the most important way to get ahead in the organization. This can be valuable if the mid-level managers find useful ways to contribute to the performance of the organization. It can be disastrous if the managerial ranks simply provide a refuge for officers who wish to flee the rigors of operating at the work face of the organization on the street where the value of policing is realized.

These organizational forms also tend to centralize decision making in police organizations—at least at the formal level. One reason for this is the symbolism of tight control and command. In this imagery, each officer is the embodiment of the will of the chief of police, whose desires about how the police should behave are set forth in the organization's manual of policies and procedures and are enforced by the ranks of mid-level managers. The department behaves in a uniform and correct manner and thereby reassures citizens that the law is applied equally and properly in individual cases.

The organizational ideology of central control is made concrete and practical insofar as officers look to higher levels of the organization for authorization to take action, and insofar as it encourages those at higher levels to take responsibility for the actions of subordinates. Because there are a great many middle managers who conceive of their jobs as controlling the conduct of lower level officers, there is always someone of higher rank from whom a lower level officer can obtain guidance. Moreover, officers have an incentive to seek guidance because such consultation will absolve them of any blame if the approved action goes sour. It is these dynamics that tend to push formal decision making toward the center in police organizations.

The concept of decentralization, on the other hand, is often misunderstood in a police organization. For some, decentralization means having substations and mini-stations in which patrol officers and investigators work. The presence or absence of these facilities is often used as a basis for describing whether the organization is decentralized or not.

What is meant by decentralization here is something different. A decentralized organization is one in which initiative, decisions and responsibility are pushed down to the lowest possible level of the organization. In a decentralized organization, street-level officers have much greater freedom to make decisions about what work should be done to contribute to the overall objectives of the organization and how that work should get done.

The advantages of decentralization are essentially three. First, it frees higher level managers from having to spend all their time and intellectual energy on pressing operational matters, and thereby enables them to concentrate on making those strategic investments that will improve the organization's capabilities to perform in the future. Second, operational decisions are arguably improved because they are more timely and are made by people who are closer to the facts of the situation, though there is the risk that such people are less skilled and experienced than their immediate supervisor. Third, by pushing responsibility and initiative downward in the organization, more people are challenged to be creative and useful in the organization. That generally results in higher morale and greater opportunity to spot and develop talent in the organization.[7]

Recently, doubts have arisen about whether the current preference for centralized over decentralized structures in police departments should be continued. The principal reason to doubt the wisdom of centralization is that the reality of police operations departs radically from the image of nondiscretionary decision making in routine cases and centralized decision making in novel circumstances. The operational reality in most police departments is that officers and investigators operating on the street confront many nonroutine situations.[8] For example, they must decide whether to arrest and whether to use force largely on their own. Situations develop sufficiently quickly that officers cannot always ask for approval in advance. Moreover, many situations are unique, and as such are not covered by existing policies and procedures. Officers address such situations using a great deal of informal discretion. Thus the quality of policing generally depends on the initiative, values and discretion of officers rather than on the completeness of the policies and procedures and the closeness with which they are supervised. If this is true, it might be valuable to a police organization to encourage and use the initiative and discretion of officers rather than try to eliminate it.

A second reason to be concerned about the appropriateness of centralized, hierarchical structures is that their very form works against police aspirations for professional status. A professional is one who can be trusted to exercise discretion for the benefit of society on the basis of his or her accumulated expertise and commitment to the values that guide the profession. Professionals are not seen as requiring close supervision. As a result, the structure of the organizations they inhabit are generally quite flat. Professionals are held accountable through peer evaluations of their performance after the fact rather than through prior authorization and close supervision by their superiors. The hierarchical, centralized structures are characteristic of organizations in which the workers cannot be entirely trusted either because they lack the necessary expertise and technical imagination or because they cannot be relied upon to have the proper values in taking action.

A third factor undermining confidence in these hierarchical forms is simply that they create a great deal of waste with layers of mid-level managers whose functions are obscure. It is by no means clear what a lieutenant or sergeant is supposed to do in a police department.[9] One can imagine a world in which lieutenants became mid-level managers not simply by writing out the shift schedule and manning the station house, but by proposing tactical solutions to problems, developing innovations with respect to police operations or working with community groups to identify their priorities. One can imagine sergeants assuming primary responsibilities for training and developing officers—coaching them on how to do their jobs better rather than overseeing their activities and insisting that they do the jobs just as the book demands, or just as the sergeant prefers. In today's police organizations, however, it is fairly rare for mid-level managers to take on these kinds of responsibilities. Moreover, it is not at all clear that we need as many mid-level managers as we seem to have to fulfill these functions.

If police organizations were to shift to flatter, more decentralized organizational forms to reflect the operational reality of initiative and discretionary decision making in the organization's front lines, police executives would have to solve two important problems arising from the abandonment of the traditional form. First, police executives would have to find some other way of assuring citizens that the officers would remain under control and that their actions would be guided by the proper public values now encapsulated in formal policies and procedures. Second, police executives would have to develop other career paths through the organization (other than up through the rank structure) in order to maintain the commitment and motivation of officers over the course of a career in the department.

The section on controlling later in this chapter presents some alternative ways of maintaining the accountability of officers other than close operational supervision, namely, the use of training, an emphasis on values and after-the-fact accountability for performance rather than before-the-fact approval. The section on staffing, which follows next, presents a solution to the career path issue, namely, allowing people to advance to higher status and higher pay by advancing through skill levels rather than through ranks.

Staffing

Staffing today's police organization is a critically important managerial function. The average police department devotes about 80% of its budget to personnel. Moreover, the events that turn out to be decisive in influencing the public's perception of the police generally turn on the quality of judgment that individual officers show in tough situations and their manner in executing routine functions. Staffing is also a complex function. It encompasses a number of major subfunctions—human resource planning, recruitment and selection, recruit training, in-service training, evaluation and promotion and career development--each of which is discussed below.

Human Resource Planning

Human resource planning establishes the framework for meeting the future personnel needs of the organization. It requires managers to calculate how many employees will be needed, when and with what skills and experience. The human resource plan must be consistent with the structure of the organization, which sets out the number of positions of various types, and with the budget, which imposes limits on either personnel expenditures of various kinds or the total positions to be filled. In addition, the human resource plan must take into account the department's experience with personnel turnover. Perhaps most important, it must examine how much investment in the form of training and developmental assignments will be required to ensure the quality of the people the organization needs.

A particularly important and sensitive issue that must be dealt with in the context of human resource planning (as well as in human resource management) is the scope and character of the department's affirmative action efforts. Affirmative action is a key issue in the management of police departments for at least three reasons.

First, police departments are under legal requirements to engage in effective affirmative action programs.[10] These requirements are monitored by vigilant representatives of minority groups and by the courts. As law enforcement agencies, it is particularly important that the police be in compliance with the law.

Second, legal requirements notwithstanding, the police should be interested in affirmative action for ethical and practical reasons. Every public organization, and particularly those that stand for fairness, have a moral obligation to help minority groups and women overcome the legacy of past discrimination.[11] The practical reason is that the police, perhaps more than any other public agency, have an interest in reflecting the characteristics of the populations they serve. The police are particularly vulnerable, for example, to being seen as an "occupying army" if they are largely white and the communities they police are not.[12] And, as we have been learning, the police are particularly dependent on close relations with the communities they serve. Thus, police departments must practice affirmative action to ensure adequate representation of minorities.

Third, to some degree, a department's commitment to affirmative action, and its skill in recruiting or developing minority police officers, is an important strategic device for changing the style of policing in a city. One of the principal thrusts of the movement to professionalize policing has been to raise standards for recruitment, particularly educational standards. For many, that effort seems to conflict with the goals of affirmative action because minorities have historically had fewer opportunities for higher education than whites. This presents police executives with a cruel dilemma. Holding to high standards of recruitment may cause them and the department to be viewed as not being committed to affirmative action goals. But if the department is not representative of the community, it will be deprived both of the information and perspective on policing that minority candidates can bring and of the important links that they can establish with minority communities. If, on the other hand, standards are relaxed to achieve affirmative action objectives, they run the risk that the officers they recruit will lack the skills, values and judgment required to make a first-rate police officer.

Resolution of this dilemma will not be easy. Educational level is thought to be an important standard by most police executives even though only 14% of the police agencies serving populations greater than 50,000 have educational requirements beyond high school. The primary reason for not increasing educational standards is fear that affirmative action goals will not be met.

Some departments have worked to resolve this dilemma by developing special programs to recruit police at the high school level. These programs provide part-time jobs and tuition at community colleges for students who have strong aptitudes and some inclination toward policing.[13] Such programs have helped departments elevate their educational standards without negatively affecting affirmative action objectives. Others have targeted minority students in law enforcement programs on college campuses and have made special efforts to recruit at minority colleges.

Deciding exactly how to reach affirmative action objectives reveals the importance of human resource planning to the strategic purposes of the organization. The planning process must help the organization see that affirmative action is not an awkward, external constraint, but a strategically significant issue for the organization. The organization must find a way to harmonize two apparently conflicting goals—improving educational levels and increasing the number of minorities within police departments. The solution lies in developing innovative ways to improve other aspects of the personnel system: recruitment, selection and development.

Recruitment and Selection

Recruitment and selection have been particularly difficult for police departments in recent years. On average, police agencies screen about ten candidates for every one they hire. Police often point to this ratio with pride, believing it indicates the attractiveness of policing as a profession and the stringency of current standards. But this ratio may also indicate unfocused recruiting programs. In fact, most police departments do not recruit—they just select from among those who apply. A recent survey of police officers in California indicates that only one in eight was influenced in his or her choice of departments by a recruiter.

In the future, the one-in-ten ratio is likely to grow if present methods are continued. The police are finding it increasingly difficult to fill positions with qualified applicants. Population projections indicate the size of the age groups from which the police ordinarily recruit will decline through the late 1990s. Moreover, many of those now applying to police departments come with an important handicap: a record of prior drug use or indications of current drug use. Departments across the nation report that as many as three-quarters of their applicants admit to having experimented with drugs at some point in their lives.[14] This admission currently disqualifies many applicants from further consideration.

Two proposals could radically alter police capacities to recruit large numbers of highly qualified candidates. One is the idea of a police cadet corps which would provide individuals with a free college education in return for serving as a police officer.[15] The second is to change the occupational status of policing by truly professionalizing police departments, that is, flattening police organizations dramatically, increasing the discretion of officers and increasing pay. It is possible that many people who now see policing as a "blue-collar" job would be attracted if it became a "white-collar" job. There is certainly enough challenge and importance in the job to qualify it for white-collar status.

Recruit Training

Once a department hires new officers, it has the responsibility to train them to carry out their new duties. One of the largest training investments police agencies make is at entry level. This training involves from three to six months of classroom training, followed by one to three months in the field.[16] Throughout this period, the officer is usually on probation, and performance is closely monitored for signs of unusual aptitude or disability in performing the tasks that police officers must perform. In this sense, entry level training is an extension of the selection and screening function.

The cost of this process is very high, and departments have begun to seek less expensive alternatives. Minnesota has an innovative plan that requires officers to be certified by the state as possessing certain skills before the officer can be employed.[17] The plan requires, among other things, that the applicant complete most of the training in state-supported schools at his or her expense. Although the police department must still orient new officers to its particular methods and equipment, the cost of training to the department is much reduced. In Florida, individuals may attend state-certified training academies on their own or under the sponsorship of a police department.[18]

Programs like these are still exceptions to the norm. They do reduce the cost to police departments of training new officers, but they also present some obstacles. One negative aspect of these "self-serve" training programs is they may make it harder rather than easier for the police to recruit candidates from poor communities. Unless scholarships are available, some candidates may turn to other careers because they are unable to pay for their training to be police officers.

In-Service Training

Following the initial training period, police departments must continue to provide employees with training and developmental opportunities so they can hone their skills, add to their competencies and prepare themselves for advancement. Such efforts are valued by employees because they provide new challenges, a new sense of mastery and opportunities for higher pay, greater autonomy and more responsibility. They also break up the monotony of continuously performing the same job. Such efforts serve the interests of the department by enriching the variety of employee skills, increasing the department's flexibility, enhancing motivation and morale and improving management.

Currently, most departments provide such training inside the department or at statewide criminal justice training facilities.[19] Most of the programs focus on the traditional technical skills of policing: taking fingerprints, presenting evidence in court, conducting drug investigations, managing informants, undertaking financial investigations, understanding the law of search and seizure and using new equipment.[20]

Recently, departments have begun training their employees in nontraditional police methods. They have begun offering training in crime analysis, intelligence operations and problem-solving methods. In addition, sessions on community and press relations are being included in training programs.

But among the most important changes is an increased concern for management training, particularly for managers at the higher levels of the department. This interest in managerial training emerges from a recognition that mastery of the techniques of policing and long experience as a police officer do not necessarily prepare a person to be the leader of a police organization. Even if a person has performed well in supervisory roles, he or she is not necessarily equipped to become an innovative mid-level manager or the chief executive officer of a department.

To be an effective manager, a police executive officer must be able to blend the contributions that are made by each of the functional specialties within the department.[21] This means understanding budgeting, cost accounting and press relations as well as the management of patrol operations, hostage situations and complex drug investigations. Even more important, it means creating conditions in the department in which the functional specialties can work together effectively. A police manager also must be capable of having a vision of the future that is realistic but challenging, and of communicating that vision effectively both outside and inside the department. A police manager must also be capable of managing processes of innovation, change and learning within the department.

To develop these newly appreciated managerial skills, police departments have often had to look outside their departments. The opportunities for those seeking management training range from graduate degree programs in local colleges and universities to national programs designed specifically for the law enforcement community. The Federal Bureau of Investigation sponsors a number of such programs, including the FBI National Academy, the Law Enforcement Executive Development Seminar, and the National Executive Institute. The Southern Police Institute and Northwestern University also offer programs that reach national audiences. The Police Executive Research Forum has sponsored the Senior Management Institute for Police since 1981. The three-week program is conducted in conjunction with the faculty from John F. Kennedy School of Government at Harvard University.

While the national training programs make a great contribution, they fall far short of meeting the national demand for highly qualified managerial training. This has led to the development of programs at the state level. One of the most well known is the California Command College. This highly selective program lasts for two years and requires participants to do independent research on some aspect of policing and the future. Other states like Florida, Illinois, Ohio and Texas are developing new programs aimed at the management and executive levels.

In other areas, departments have been able to make effective use of private corporations that have been willing to include police managers in their training programs.

"Operation Bootstrap," initiated by the Washington State Police and Sheriff's Associations, has grown into a national program that has provided training opportunities for police officers over the past few years. Such programs have not only developed the managerial skills of police managers, but enhanced their identification with the managerial function and increased their self-confidence.

On-the-job training is also a critical supplement to outside programs for police managers and supervisors. Four techniques are commonly used: coaching, job rotation, apprenticeships and planned work activity.

Perhaps the most effective technique is "coaching."[22] Coaching provides daily opportunities to solve managerial and supervisory challenges in the work setting. The method is a little like clinical training for physicians. It requires the trainee to define and resolve actual operating situations and then discuss his or her methods with the coach. If this method is to be successful, coaches and trainees must be carefully matched. Coaches may also have to be trained. A department that makes good use of this method can make rapid strides in developing an effective cadre of managers and supervisors. This method also fosters a spirit of cooperation and mutual learning among an organization's top managers.

The second method of training managers on the job depends on job rotation.[23] Managerial and supervisory personnel are systematically shifted among key jobs in the organization to familiarize them with the different functions of the organization. These programs widen skills and perspectives. They also enable managers to build up networks of personal relations across entire organizations that will increase their abilities to make things happen across organizational boundaries.[24]

The third method is to apprentice those judged to have executive potential to the senior commanders of the organization. The Kansas City Police Department, for example, assigned young police officers to its Planning and Research Division to bring them into contact with the perspectives, problems and methods of Chief Clarence Kelley.[25]

The fourth method is the use of planned work activity. This involves assigning individuals to a committee, task force or major project that is essential to the strategic development of the organization. In recent years, a good example of this sort of assignment has been the task of managing a department's efforts to win national accreditation. Many individuals assigned this task have been promoted, and for some, it has been a springboard for becoming a police chief.

The organizational structure of the police department has important implications for the types of opportunities the organization has to develop its officers as general managers. A functional organizational structure forces departments to use methods such as job rotation or planned work activity to test and develop the general managers of the organization. The reason is that in a functional organization, one tends to become a high-level manager by mastering the techniques of one's function. The head of administration and management might be the only top-level executive in a police department who understands budgeting and cost accounting and knows how resources flow through the department. The head of the narcotics division may be the only top-level official who understands financial investigations and forfeiture laws.

To some extent, having managers who understand their specialties extremely well is a great advantage for an organization. They represent a great technical resource and are often a source of professional pride and reputation for the department. But there is often a price to be paid as well. They tend to think in somewhat parochial rather than organizational terms, and defend their function to the death in budget debates. In addition, they tend to think of management not in terms of teamwork or developing their subordinates, but in terms of supervising people and telling them how to do the job right. This tends to stunt the organization's development. The only way to break down these tendencies is to force people to work in other jobs or to give them assignments that force them to operate across functions. That is why job rotation and special assignments are particularly important in functionally specialized organizations.

In geographically organized departments, where there are subordinate units that include a variety of functional specialties, however, departments can rely on coaching and apprenticeships. The reason is that there are far more positions in the department that resemble general management positions. In a functional organization, only the chief has to integrate functions. In a geographically decentralized organization, many people must integrate diverse functions on a small scale. That is what general management is all about.

Performance Evaluation

Performance evaluation is a key instrument of personnel policy because it gives employees guidance about what the organization thinks is important to achieve, provides incentives for them to contribute to organizational goals and creates a record of accomplishment that can be used in making promotional decisions. Despite the importance of the function, few departments perform it well.[26]

The difficulty arises right at the start: it is by no means clear what aspects of performance should be measured or how. This basic problem exists at all levels of an organization. At the lower levels, the emphasis is on "bean counting," that is, on the number of tickets written, calls answered, arrests made. Little consideration is given to how well the jobs were done or to how they relate to the overall objectives of the organization.[27] The only virtue of such measures is that the activity being measured can be objectively verified and easily quantified. These measures may also reveal something of the energy and initiative of officers.[28] But that is about all.

At higher levels of the organization, the "bean counting" continues as police executives and their overseers count reported crime rates, arrest rates, clearance rates and response times. This focus on crime-related statistics ignores other important police functions, such as traffic safety, fear reduction and drug abuse prevention. Efforts have been made over the years to resolve the issue of how best to measure police effectiveness, or the value the police create for the community, but they have met with little success.[29] Bean counting has its place in policing, but the emphasis must be shifted to developing and using other measures that more accurately reflect the effectiveness of the police.

A particularly troubling deficiency in police departments is the lack of any specific systems for monitoring the performance of mid-level managers and supervisors. Under traditional systems, police officers reach these jobs by passing written examinations that test their knowledge of police management methods. Thereafter, they are rarely evaluated on a regular basis. The only time their performance is examined is when they apply for higher positions.

Because of the lack of formal systems, it is hard to know exactly what police departments expect of their mid-level managers. In general, it seems that they are expected to show up for work get their subordinates also to show up for work, oversee their subordinates' work to ensure that they follow the appropriate procedures, report any problems to higher level officials and try to avoid disastrous mistakes and stave off corruption among their subordinates. These are the basic supervisory functions.

An alternative view of a manager's responsibility would focus on functions beyond this image of effective supervision. It would be concerned about the effective performance of the organization as well as its compliance with operating procedures. Indeed, in some cases, successful performance of a task might require an action that differed from the one prescribed by rules. In that situation, a manager might be authorized to take the action that makes sense in his or her judgment and to give permission to subordinates to operate outside the rules. Managers should also be responsible for innovations in an organization's activities. And they might also be held responsible for the development of their subordinates' skills. In short, what distinguishes a manager from a supervisor is a concern for performance, innovation and personnel development. It is in these terms that managers should be evaluated.

Promotion and Career Development

The final aspect of staffing to be addressed is the system of promotion and career development. This system provides some of the most important incentives for people to join and work hard in an organization. It is also important because the operation of this system affects everyone's view of the fairness of the organization.

The dominant method still used in police departments to evaluate people for promotion is standardized written tests and interviews.[30] Although these techniques are useful in measuring a candidate's knowledge, they are limited in determining how skillful the candidate is in applying knowledge on the job. Some departments have begun to supplement these traditional methods with the use of assessment centers.[31] Assessment centers rely on simulations of job-related situations and assessments of performance by several observers trained to be objective in evaluating the performance of candidates. This method also has its limitations, but it at least offers some insight into how candidates would actually perform in a job.

An alternative method of making promotional decisions is to base the decisions on demonstrated performance. Past performance is generally the best predictor of future performance, yet police departments do not position themselves to exploit that fact by accurately recording past performance. Thus, the failure of the performance appraisal system becomes the failure of the promotional system as well.

Two key issues in promotion/career advancement warrant attention. The first is the fact that most police departments hold out only two paths for police officers to enhance their pay, working conditions and status: they can seek promotion to a higher rank, or they can transfer to the detective bureau. This fact encourages police officers with ambition and initiative to flee from the primary work face of the organization—patrol operations. If police departments are to shift to strategies of policing that require more of patrol officers, and that truly professionalize policing, they will have to develop ways for officers to enhance their status, pay and working conditions while remaining on the street. In effect, what is needed is a system that rewards advancement through *skill* levels in the same job as much or more than it rewards advancement through *ranks*. One concrete idea consistent with this general thrust is the proposal to establish ranks of "master patrol officers," who might be paid as much as sergeants or lieutenants.

The second issue is that of lateral entry. Few police departments consider candidates for promotion from outside the department. There is great resistance to this practice among police officers who do not want their promotional opportunities jeopardized, and serious technical problems associated with pension mobility would have to be overcome. Nevertheless, the lack of circulation and mobility of police officers across the nation's departments stunts the development of policing. The organizations become insular and parochial. Innovations are not widely diffused. Promotional opportunities come to rely more on personal relationships than demonstrated performance. Individuals in organizations become afraid to leave. The flow of opportunities and new ideas dries up.

Controlling

The third key managerial function that police managers must perform is controlling the resources and operations of their departments and accounting for the costs and results of their efforts to external authorities. As noted earlier, the two key resources that police executives are responsible for are the public money entrusted to them and the authority vested in police officers.

Financial Control

The principal mechanisms for controlling an organization's financial resources are the budget and the cost-accounting system.[32] The budget sets out a planned use of expenditures for an organization and is approved annually by a higher political authority. The cost-accounting system measures the flow of expenditures through the organization and attributes them to particular activities.

Police executives must address three major issues associated with financial control systems: (1) how the budget should be developed, (2) how the budget can be used to reflect not only operational expenditures but also key investments needed to improve an organization's future performance and (3) how organizational activities and accomplishments should be measured and attributed to particular costs centers.

In most police departments, budgets are prepared by civilians in administrative support units. The principal line commanders of the organization are often not directly involved. In some cases, the chief executive is not even significantly involved. To the extent that mid-level managers are involved in the process, they focus their attention on staffing levels and small equipment items in the units for which they are responsible.

This kind of budgeting system makes sense in an organization that thinks about its activities in terms of staffing existing organizational units. It does not make sense in an organization that focuses on identifying problems to be solved. In an organization that focuses on identifying and solving problems for the community, the managers must constantly be thinking about specific projects to be undertaken, as well as about how to fill existing posts. Ideas about problems to be addressed become claimants on the organization's resources, however, and thus should be reflected in budgeting decisions. To the extent that the projects propose solutions to problems that are important to those who oversee police departments, they may garner more resources for the police department. In a problem-solving department, then, the budgeting process will be more participatory and "bottom-up" than in a traditional department.

Most budgeting systems in police departments are also designed as expense budgets that show how resources will be used that year to sustain certain levels and kinds of activities. Most police departments also have expenses that are reflected in the city's capital budget, including expenditures on new police facilities. What is not often recognized in these budgets, however, is a kind of expenditure that is crucially important in organizations that are labor intensive rather than capital intensive and are going through periods of innovation. These are investments in organizational capabilities that do not look like capital expenditures because they do not involve bricks and mortar, or even very large amounts of money. Nonetheless these outlays function as investments because they are expenditures made now whose value will be realized in the enhanced future performance of the organization. Such expenditures could include the specialized training required to reorient a department from one kind of policing to another, the redesign of computer-aided dispatching systems to give as much emphasis to maintaining beat integrity as to minimizing response times[33] or the documentation of experimental approaches to dealing with commonly encountered police problems, such as domestic disputes.

The difficulty in identifying these kinds of expenditures in the ordinary budgets of police departments means that managers and overseers cannot really see the magnitudes of these investments. Some important investments and innovations come plainly marked, such as experimental grants that are funded by outside sources and that include special requirements for evaluation. But there is no routine way to observe, manage or plead for funds to change the way the police department operates. The budget reinforces the assumption that the most effective programmatic and technological means for accomplishing purposes are not only already well known but also already incorporated in police department operations.

The third important problem with current budgeting and cost-accounting systems is that they are relatively weak in measuring the results of police department's operations and in attributing costs to the different results.

97

Consequently, it is hard for police executives and their overseers to determine how much value has been created by police activities and which activities were particularly valuable.

As noted above, police departments generally measure their results in terms of the number of reported crimes, the reported crimes cleared by arrest, the overall number of arrests for different kinds of crime and the speed of their response to calls for service.[34] Some of these measures are relevant to judging effectiveness because they are related to the desired outcomes of public policing (e.g., the number of reported crimes). Others are less relevant to judging efficiency because they measure only the organization's outputs (e.g., arrests and response rates).[35]

Some analysts of police departments make a strong argument for relying only on outcome measures, such as reduced crime, to assess the value created by police departments. They argue that it is these anticipated results that define the value of the police department, and it is only the demonstration of such results that could justify continued expenditures.[36] From a managerial perspective, however, outcome measures have some important disadvantages. It is possible, for example, that the value created by a police department for its citizens is not well captured by the impact of the police department on levels of crime. It might be as important that the police reduce fear and citizen reliance on their own self-defense, and respond competently to the wide variety of social and medical emergencies that occur among the population. There are some, for example, who see the police as an important health-protecting agency, because the police can do something about the things that kill young people, namely, driving recklessly, drinking, taking drugs and engaging in gang violence.[37]

Even if one had properly defined the value created by police organizations, there is still the enormous problem of measuring the police contribution to whatever results occur. There are technical problems in measuring levels of crime and their changes from year to year.[38] In addition, it is very difficult to attribute changes in crime levels to the police because many things other than police operations affect these numbers. Finally, it is expensive to collect the data and do the analyses that attempt to measure the impact of police agencies on criminal victimization. As a result, these studies are not done often.

These observations suggest that outcome measurement alone cannot be the managerial answer to assessing the value of police operations. The measurement of the quantity and quality of *outputs*, such as clearances, arrests and response times, has some important advantages over *outcome* measurement. Data on outputs can be easily collected on a regular basis, accumulated for many different subordinate units and attributed directly to the actions of particular managers in police departments. These features make output measures much more managerially valuable than outcome measures, for they can be tied directly to a system of managerial accountability and control.

Output measures have two key weaknesses, however. The first is that they are not direct measures of the value that police departments produce, even though they may be related to the ultimate purposes of the organization. But if they are, it is through a theory about the overall purposes of the police and the most effective means for achieving those purposes. For example, clearances by arrest are thought to be important crime-fighting tools because it would seem that crime could be effectively controlled by deterring and incapacitating criminal offenders. If that theory is correct, then measuring arrests and successful prosecutions is almost as good as measuring direct reductions in crime. If, however, that theory is wrong, or if it depends on actions taken by others in the system (e.g., prosecutors, judges and prison wardens), then it is by no means clear that the number of arrests is a measure of police value.

The second weakness is far easier to repair. In most departments, the standard measures of organizational output are not closely audited. Clearance rates are notoriously unreliable. Even arrest data are suspect. As a result, it is hard for police executives or their overseers to rely on these data.

Recently, as police executives have been rethinking the mission and operations of police departments, they have begun tinkering with the systems that measure their efficiency and effectiveness. Some executives have begun to describe reported crimes in terms of precipitating cause, time, location and losses to victims, as well as the relationship between victims and offenders. Their purpose is to see whether there are some kinds of crime that police can affect more than others.[39] Other executives, aware that large amounts of crime go unreported and concerned about levels of fear and citizen perceptions of the quality of police services, have begun to use annual community surveys to see how their organization is affecting underlying levels of crime and fear.[40] Some executives are beginning to think about surveying people who have called the police, to determine their level of satisfaction with the police response. These are all new ways to think about and measure the value produced by police departments for their communities.

Managing the Use of Authority

Budgeting and cost-accounting systems measure an organization's use of the *financial* resources entrusted to it. They do not measure the care, efficiency or effectiveness with which the police use the *authority* granted to them. Indeed, the systems used for managing the police use of authority tend to be quite different from those used for managing the department's use of money.

The most common device for controlling the use of authority is the establishment of internal policies and procedures. These are inculcated through recruit and in-service training. They are reinforced through close supervision by the line commanders of the organization and by the threat of investigation by the department's internal affairs unit.[41] The internal affairs unit is typically set up to receive and investigate complaints or allegations of misconduct from sources inside and outside the department. If the complaints or allegations are found to be justified, cases against officers will be referred either for internal disciplinary proceedings or for criminal prosecution. In some departments, the internal affairs unit engages in proactive efforts to identify instances of misconduct, on the grounds that citizens might be afraid to come forward with an allegation against a police officer even if it were warranted.[42] This is relatively rare, however.

Many local governments, having decided that internal control procedures do not adequately protect citizens from police misconduct nor provide sufficiently accurate information about the extent of police misconduct, have established external agencies to oversee the police. Some of these agencies take the form of Civilian Complaint Review Boards.[43] Others are simply an ombudsman's office.[44]

One of the most powerful controls over police abuse of authority, however, is the growing threat of civil liability.[45] Citizens who are abused by the police may sue them. They may even be able to get help in investigating instances of police misconduct by calling on the Federal Bureau of Investigation which has the responsibility for investigating allegations of civil rights violations. Citizens may also be able to sue in federal court. So far, the local government as a whole has assumed the liability for the misconduct of police officers. But the financial costs of such actions have been rising, and that has brought new pressures from the powerful financial agencies on local governments to minimize police misconduct.[46]

The effort to account for and control the use of police authority is, in an important sense, still in its infancy. For a long time, the police have not thought of their authority as a resource that it was their duty to husband — to use efficiently and fairly. They have, instead, assumed that it was theirs to command. What a generation of police reform has taught us is that legitimate authority is a very precious asset to a police department, and if the public is to trust the police use of that resource, and therefore make more of it available to the professionals they rely on to safeguard their lives and property from criminal attack, then the police must be able to control and account for its use.

Summary

The administrative systems of police departments have been adapted to fit the current strategy of policing. The centralized, functionally dominated organizational structures have separated the police from local political influences, focused their attention on the development of specialized functional capabilities and encouraged them to take only a jurisdiction-wide perspective on problems. The heavy emphasis on eligibility standards and technical training has been used to elevate the professionalism of the police. The financial control systems have been placed in the hands of specialists, in keeping with the overall functional organization of the department. And the police have evaluated themselves largely in terms of crime-related indicators of success. All this is quite consistent with a strategy of professional crime fighting.

If the strategy of policing were to change in the direction of community policing or problem-oriented policing, however, these administrative systems would have to be substantially altered.[47] The administrative structure would have to be changed from a functional orientation to a geographic one to enable the police to develop the rapport they need with local community groups. The centralized decision-making structure would have to yield to a much flatter, more decentralized style to acknowledge the reality of the organization's dependence on the initiative and discretion of its front-line officers, and to exploit their skills. The training emphasis would have to shift from academy-based training to clinical, on-the-job training. Control of officers would have to change from a system of rules enforced by close supervision and prior authorization of action to a system of values supported by the organization's culture and evaluation of officers' actions after the fact. The financial systems would have to reflect the fact that the organization's work changes from year to year, and that the organization must make investments in new capabilities rather than simply relying on past knowledge and techniques. Departments would also have to develop new means of evaluating police services. And finally, the departments would have to develop systems that monitor the ways in which they are using the authority entrusted to them, and in particular whether force and authority are being used fairly and economically.

These changes in administrative systems would change the strategy of policing, as well as reflect a shift in philosophy. How an executive could make such changes in an organization committed to the reform strategy of policing is the subject of the next chapter.

Chapter 5

Leadership and the Future of Policing

Throughout, this essay has surveyed the opportunities and challenges facing police agencies from the perspective of the chief. It has imputed to the chief a particular point of view—the perspective characteristic of a chief executive officer of a value-seeking enterprise. It has implicitly assumed that a police chief has the discretion to envision alternative, higher value uses of the department and to invoke the power of the chief's office to move the department toward those uses. This perspective assumes a certain style of police leadership that is not necessarily the style of leadership that is now expected of police executives, nor common among them. Indeed, most police executives think of their leadership obligations in quite different terms.

Images of Police Leadership

Probably a significant number of police executives think of themselves as "stewards" of their organizations. In this conception, the organization is seen as a well-developed piece of machinery that needs nothing more than routine maintenance to keep it functioning. No urgent design changes are required. The task of the executive is to keep the organization on an even keel. The executive must concentrate on ensuring that reasonable budgetary growth is sustained so that the organization can continue its work. He or she must protect the autonomy of the organization against those who seek to influence it. The executive seeks to reassure the officers that the system of promotion and advancement is fair and that, if they behave themselves, they can count on a successful career in the organization. The implicit assumption is that the organization does not really belong to the chief executive; he or she is simply presiding over its operations for a while.

A slightly more activist stance is taken by the larger number of police executives who think of themselves as "commanders" of their organizations. These executives exert more hands-on control of their organizations than stewards do. They run lines of tension throughout their organizations through the sustained, activist oversight of police operations. Indeed, in some particularly thorny situations, they assume direct operational command of the police response. They demand a great deal in terms of loyalty, competence and effort from their subordinates, and although their judgments are often seen as sudden and arbitrary, they try to be fair. They are aggressive supporters of the police among external groups, and they guard their prerogatives of command quite jealously. The implicit assumption of these executives is that the organization knows the right thing to do, but it must be made to do the right thing by the force of the manager's oversight and commitment.

Neither of these images is quite like the image of a police "executive." Neither the "steward" nor the "commander" feels responsible for broad, strategic thinking about how the organization's value to society can be maximized. They both think that the answer to that question has been given. Neither the steward nor the commander imagines significant changes in the operating procedures or administrative relations that characterize the department. The steward relies on tradition and cumulative operational experience codified in standard operating procedures to guide the department. The commander relies on his or her own substantive knowledge and force of personality. Neither imagines that frequent innovations are required, or that those innovations might come from subordinates. Neither is much inclined to be influenced by external demands on the organization. Each sees external demands as threats to be warded off rather than as important sources of information about how the organizations might best be used. In short, neither stewards nor commanders are inclined toward risky, strategic changes in the mission and operations of police agencies.

Resistance to Change

It is not particularly surprising that there are relatively few strategic leaders of police departments. Police chiefs who adopt this style of leadership automatically assume a heavy burden of responsibility. They essentially announce that, in their opinion, significant changes in the direction and operations of the organization are required, and that they are determined to bring them about. This stance naturally focuses attention on them and makes them the target of any opposition that might arise. It also exposes them to the special criticism that they are arrogant, self-seeking grandstanders vying for public attention. That opposition will arise to police executives such as these is virtually guaranteed. The reason is essentially that expectations have accumulated inside and outside the organization about how the organization will be run and these expectations will invariably come into conflict with a strategic police executive.

Inside the organization, employees have made investments in themselves and commitments to one another, based on the expectation that the organization will continue to operate as it has in the past. Those investments and commitments are an important source of security in a world that otherwise looks quite uncertain and threatening. They operate as a kind of wealth for the employees— something that the employees can count on and that insulates them from disaster. When an executive announces a strategic change in the organization, or acts in a way that portends such a change, he or she implicitly strips away the wealth and security that the employees have developed. They, quite naturally, become upset and worried. Even those employees who might benefit from the proposed changes will not necessarily see this opportunity at the outset. The potential gains will be discounted by the uncertainty about whether the proposed changes will actually occur, and whether they will really be valuable to the employees.

Outside the organization, in the mayor's office, editorial boards and civic associations, people pay less attention. But they, too, have expectations about how the police department is supposed to be operated and managed. One of their ideas is that things should go smoothly, and there should not be turmoil. Another is that there should be widespread respect for the professional competence of the person who leads the organization. It is these expectations that allow them not to have to think too much about policing and to pay attention to other business. They may also have an expectation that the fundamental job of the police is to be professional crime fighters. If these expectations are upset—if it appears that there is turmoil in the department and that the turmoil is being created by an executive who does not understand his job or the mission of the police—then the outsiders will intervene. The intervention will often be to remove the chief so that things can get back to normal.

The insiders know this. They also have relatively easy ways of mobilizing the outsiders. There is often a police union that can complain loudly about the changes planned or occurring within the department. The detectives often have quite easy access to police reporters, who can produce stories about declining morale and a loss of professional competence as a result of changes the chief is making. Thus, subordinates, in alliance with outsiders, can oust a chief who demands changes that are unpopular. Indeed, it is probably true that more police executives have been fired by their subordinates than by their mayors.

Overcoming Resistance

Given the power of rigid expectations to constrain a chief's room for maneuvering, it is not surprising that the most important changes in police departments have occurred in the midst of crises, for example, in the aftermath of a riot, a corruption scandal or a notorious breakdown in operational efficiency.[1] Crises seem to be important in police reform precisely because they unsettle expectations about how the police should behave. In this sense, crises might be seen as the public sector equivalent of private sector bankruptcies.

The popular image of a bankruptcy is one in which a company's assets are seized by its creditors and sold off to retire as much of the debt of the organization as possible. But that is not usually what happens. Often what happens is that the firm is "restructured" into a profit-making enterprise. Old activities that were not profitable are sold off. Inefficient managerial and operational practices that have accumulated within the organization are rooted out. Everyone begins to work harder to have the organization succeed. Soon, the organization works itself out of bankruptcy.

What is surprising and important about these turnarounds is that management was powerless to bring them about without going into bankruptcy first. What is particularly surprising is that often the moves necessary to save the company were well known or easily ascertainable, before the company went into bankruptcy. Why didn't management make the necessary changes and avoid the pain of bankruptcy? The answer seems to be that private sector managers are as imprisoned by expectations as are public sector managers. The required changes were painful ones, and rather than face up to them and inflict the losses, the executives sought to avoid the reality of the need to make changes. Or, the executives may well have seen the necessity for change but been powerless to convince their subordinates.

This situation changes markedly when the organization is actually bankrupt. Then, the reality can no longer be avoided. Then, the expectations and commitments that so long frustrated change are liquidated by the overwhelming fact of failure. Then, resources that were unavailable because they were committed to inefficient uses are suddenly freed up. Then, the executive, far from being the source of all the problems, becomes the only person who can lead the organization out of its peril. Then, instead of fighting to maintain prerogatives and to extract more of the surplus being generated by the organization, the subordinate parts of the organization rediscover the advantages of joining in common cause.

Something like this is what happens in a police department when it encounters a problem that casts doubt on the department's ability to do its job. As the gale of public outrage and concern sweeps across the organization, expectations and assumptions are undermined. The organization begins to doubt. It looks to its leader to chart a path away from its danger. The chief is given a freer hand in directing the organization.[2] Consequently, most important strategic changes in police departments have occurred in the aftermath of dramatic performance failures that seemed to reveal an incompetent organization. For the most part, these crises have occurred naturally. Managers have not precipitated them. Indeed they have tried to forestall them as long as possible, and then were swept aside when they occurred.

If the mechanisms really operate as suggested here, there is an important message for those who would exercise strategic leadership of a police department. The most radical idea is to wait for a major crisis. Somewhat less radical is the idea that managers might use smaller crises in organizational performance to help them accomplish strategic changes. Each small crisis might provide the top-level manager a chance to intervene, to innovate, to instruct, to reallocate resources and to test his or her personnel.[3] Indeed, some business school professors have said that the principal instrument of strategic management is to "make maximum use of minimal crises."[4]

An even less radical idea is for police executives to come to understand that the expectations of the external world, created at least partly by how the organization chooses to represent itself and its activities to the community, are an important source of leverage for them in directing the activities of their organizations.[5] In this important sense, external accountability helps police executives to manage. Without external accountability, they are powerless to resist the demands of their own troops. If they give over to their own troops the power to establish the terms by which the organization will be held accountable, they forfeit all opportunity to provide strategic direction to the organization. The external demands on the organization are the only things powerful enough to dissolve the claims and expectations that develop inside the organization.

Problematic Realities

The mechanisms discussed above work to overcome resistance to change because they change the reality to which the organization must adapt if it is to survive and flourish. Crises and bankruptcies represent undeniable intrusions of reality. They require a creative, adaptive organizational response. The realities may have been there for a long time, but widely and deliberately ignored by the organization because their implications were far too threatening. It is the fundamental task of strategic leaders to uncover these realities and prepare their organizations to respond to them. No one's judgment about these matters can be sure, but at least seven key realities now facing police executives and the organizations they lead require a creative response.

First, the police are having a very tough time dealing with crime all by themselves. Moreover, it is by no means clear that the problems would disappear if prosecutors were more determined, judges harsher and jails more spacious. There are limits to what the police and the rest of the criminal justice system can do alone.

Second, effective crime control depends on an effective working partnership between the police and citizens in the communities they police. In fact, the citizens, and their determination to defend themselves and produce order in their communities, must be viewed as the first line of defense against crime and disorder. That is true even, or perhaps especially, in those communities whose capacities for self-defense now seem limited because they have been corrupted by pervasive criminality or because they have limited social and economic resources. There, the police must do more because they are more important. But the police must also find ways of developing these communities' own capacities for self-defense.

Third, public police are losing market share in the security business. As noted above, over the past decade, expenditures for private security have grown substantially while expenditures on public police have remained about constant. The number of people employed in private security has surpassed the total number of sworn officers.[6]

Fourth, public police contribute to the quality of life in their communities in many ways other than by controlling crime. Their ready availability and overall resourcefulness imply that citizens will use them for many purposes other than crime control. They are highly valued for reducing fear, restoring a sense of order and control to communities and dealing with medical and social emergencies, as well as in combatting crime. The crucial question is how easily can these other value-creating activities be fitted into the operations and culture of police departments.

Fifth, the administrative instruments now being used to ensure accountability and control of police officers cannot reliably do so. There is a sizable realm of irreducible discretion in police work. An important question is how conduct within that realm can best be managed. A further question is whether the administrative instruments that are successful in managing that realm (largely education, inculcation of values and after-the-fact evaluations of officer conduct) might be relied on more broadly to manage officers in areas where rules now dominate.

Sixth, the police are routinely held accountable for the fairness and economy with which they use force and authority, as well as money. That is what lies behind many corruption scandals and other traumatic events for police departments. The challenges are to integrate responsibility for the use of these resources into the consciousness of police departments and to find routine methods for monitoring the ways in which the police are using the resources rather than remain vulnerable to citizen outrage when a mistake occurs.

Seventh, the police are generally accountable to citizens and their political representatives. Rather than seek insulation from political interference, it is more appropriate for police agencies to make themselves more accountable to political institutions and citizens alike. Without external accountability, the police are beholden only to themselves, and police executives are powerless to challenge their own officers.

Today's police leaders are being challenged to acknowledge and find ways of accommodating these basic realities in designing the overall strategies of their organizations. Fortunately, in making these adaptations police leaders do not have to rely only on an abstract methodology. They can also rely on the examples of chiefs and organizations that are already successfully adapting to the realities that have been denied by the strategy of professional crime fighting.[7]

Conclusion

Much is changing in policing. As a result, many of the theories about the proper organization and management of police departments are changing.

This essay has sought to identify the major trends affecting the future evolution of police departments and the challenges that that evolution will present for police executives. Leadership, of course, is what is required to blaze the future trail to more effective and generally valuable police organizations. Leadership involves hazards and perils, however, for there is no clear, well-lit path to success. There is always uncertainty and turmoil as one seeks to reposition an organization for improved performance in the face of challenges that are still only dimly perceived. If this essay has been helpful to those who daily face these challenges, the authors will have fulfilled a far simpler duty.

Notes

Chapter 1. Police Orthodoxy and Strategic Management

[1]James Q. Wilson, **Bureaucracy: What Government Agencies Do and Why They Do It** (New York: Basic Books, 1989).

[2]John M. Bryson, **Strategic Planning for Public & Non-Profit Organizations** (San Francisco: Jossey-Bass, 1988).

[3]Henry Mintzberg, **The Structure of Organizations: A Synthesis of the Research** (Englewood Cliffs, NJ: Prentice-Hall, 1979).

[4]Bryson, ibid.

[5]Robert N. Anthony and R. Herzlinger, **Management Control in Nonprofit Organizations** (Homewood, IL: Irwin, 1975).

[6]O. Glenn Stahl and R. Staufenberger, eds., **Police Personnel Administration** (Washington, DC: Police Foundation, 1974). Harry P. Hatry, "Wrestling with Police Crime Control Productivity Measurement," Joan L. Wolfe and J. Heaphy, eds., **Readings on Productivity in Policing** (Washington, DC: Police Foundation, 1975).

[7]Lawrence W. Sherman, **Police Corruption: A Sociological Perspective** (New York: Anchor Books, 1974).

[8]James Q. Wilson, **The Investigators: Managing FBI and Narcotic Agents** (New York: Basic Books, 1978), pp. 163-166.

[9]George L. Kelling, "Police and Communities: The Quiet Revolution," **Perspectives on Policing**, No. 1 (Washington, DC: National Institute of Justice and Harvard University, 1988). See also Jerome Skolnick and D. Bayley, **The New Thin Blue Line: Police Innovation in Six American Cities** (New York: Free Press, 1986).

[10]An accumulating body of literature supports these conclusions. With respect to the effectiveness of random patrol, see George L. Kelling et al., **The Kansas City Preventive Patrol Experiment: A Summary Report** (Washington, DC: Police Foundation, 1974). For an evaluation of

rapid response see William G. Spelman and D. Brown, **Calling the Police: Citizen Reporting of Serious Crime** (Washington, DC: U.S. Government Printing Office, 1984); Tony Pate, A. Ferrara, R. Bowers and J. Lorence, **Police Response Time: Its Determinants and Effects** (Washington, DC: Police Foundation, 1976). On detectives and the effectiveness of retrospective investigations, see Peter W. Greenwood, J. Chaiken and J. Petersilia, **The Criminal Investigation Process** (Lexington, MA: DC Heath and Co., 1977); John Eck, **Solving Crimes: The Investigation of Burglary and Robbery** (Washington, DC: Police Executive Research Forum, 1984).

[11]Robert Wasserman and M. Moore, "Values in Policing," **Perspectives on Policing**, No. 8 (Washington, DC: National Institute of Justice and Harvard University, Nov. 1988).

[12]Mark H. Moore and R. Trojanowicz, "Corporate Strategies for Policing," **Perspectives on Policing**, No. 6 (Washington, DC: National Institute of Justice and Harvard University, Nov. 1988).

[13]Paul E. Peterson, ed., **The New Urban Reality** (Washington, DC: Brookings, 1985).

[14]Brian J. Reaves, "Police Departments in Large Cities, 1987," **Bureau of Justice Statistics Special Report** (Washington, DC: BJS, 1989), p. 7.

[15]Mark H. Moore and R. Trojanowicz, "Policing and the Fear of Crime," **Perspectives on Policing**, No. 3 (Washington, DC: National Institute of Justice, 1988).

[16]James K Stewart, "The Urban Strangler: How Crime Causes Poverty in the Inner City," **Policy Review**, 37:2-6 Summer 1986.

[17]Vera Institute of Justice, **Felony Arrests: Their Prosecution and Disposition in New York City's Courts**, rev. ed. (New York: Vera Institute; Longman, 1981).

[18]Ezra F. Vogel, **Japan as Number One: Lessons for America** (Cambridge, MA: Harvard University Press, 1979); William G. Ouchi, **Theory Z: How American Businesses Can Meet the Japanese Challenge** (Reading, MA: Addison-Wesley, 1981).

[19]Thomas J. Peters and R. Waterman, Jr., **In Search of Excellence: Lessons from America's Best-Run Companies** (New York: Harper & Row, 1982).

[20]David K. Clifford, Jr. and R. Cavanagh, **The Winning Performance: How America's High Growth Midsize Companies Succeed** (New York: Bantam Books, 1985).

[21]Ouchi, **Theory Z.** See also Harry P. Hatry and J. Greiner, **Improving the Use of Quality Circles in Police Departments** (Washington, DC: National Institute of Justice, 1986).

[22]George L. Kelling and M. Moore, "The Evolution of the Current Strategy of Policing," **Perspectives on Policing**, No. 4 (Washington, DC National Institute of Justice, 1988).

[23]An accumulating body of literature supports these conclusions. With respect to the effectiveness of random patrol, see Kelling et al., **The Kansas City Preventive Patrol Experiment.** For an evaluation of the effectiveness of directed patrol, see Tony Pate, R. Bowers and R. Parks, **Three Approaches to Criminal Apprehensions in Kansas City: An Evaluation Report** (Washington, DC: Police Foundation, 1976). For an evaluation of rapid response, see Spelman and Brown, **Calling the Police: Citizen Reporting of Serious Crime**; Pate et al., **Police Response Time.** On detectives and the effectiveness of retrospective investigations, see Greenwood, Chaiken and Petersilia, **The Criminal Investigation Process**; Eck, **Solving Crimes.**

[24]Wesley G. Skogan, "Fear of Crime and Neighborhood Change," in Albert J. Reiss, Jr. and M. Tonry, **Communities and Crime**, Vol. 8, **Crime and Justice: A Review of Research**, (Chicago: University of Chicago Press, 1986); Anthony M. Pate, M. Wycoff, W. Skogan and L. Sherman, **Reducing Fear of Crime in Houston and Newark: A Summary Report** (Washington, DC: Police Foundation, 1986).

[25]Mary Ann Wycoff, **The Role of the Municipal Police: Research as a Prelude to Changing It** (Washington, DC: Police Foundation, 1982).

[26]Lawrence W. Sherman et al., **Repeat Calls to the Police in Minneapolis** (Washington, DC: Crime Control Institute, 1987); John E. Eck and W. Spelman, **Problem Solving: Problem-Oriented Policing in Newport News** (Washington, DC: Police Executive Research Forum,

1987).

[27]Joseph Goldstein, "Police Discretion Not to Involve the Criminal Process: Low-Visibility Decisions in the Administration of Justice," **The Yale Law Journal**, 69: 543-594, 1960; James Q. Wilson, **Varieties of Police Behavior: The Management of Law and Order in Eight Communities** (Cambridge, MA: Harvard University Press, 1968).

[28]Wasserman and Moore, "Values in Policing."

[29]Kenneth R. Andrews, **The Concept of Corporate Strategy** (Chicago: Irwin, 1980), p.9.

[30]Ibid, p. iv.

[31]R. Edward Freeman, **Strategic Management: A Stakeholder Approach** (Marshall, MA: Pittman, 1984), p.10.

[32]Edith Stokey and R. Zeckhauser, **A Primer for Policy Analysis** (New York: Norton, 1978). For applications in policing, see Edward H. Kaplan, "Evaluating the Effectiveness of One-Officer versus Two-Officer Patrol Units," **Journal of Criminal Justice**, 7: 325-355.

[33]Laura Irwin Langbein, **Discovering Whether Programs Work: A Guide to Statistical Methods for Program Evaluation** (Santa Monica, CA: Goodyear, 1980). For applications in policing, see Mary Ann Wycoff, "Evaluating the Crime-Effectiveness of Municipal Police," in Jack R. Greene, ed., **Managing Police Work** (Newbury Park, CA: Sage, 1982), p.15-36; and Lawrence W. Sherman and R. Berk, "The Minneapolis Domestic Violence Experiment," **Police Foundation Reports** (Washington, DC: Police Foundation, 1984).

[34]Stokey and Zeckhauser, **A Primer for Policy Analysis.**

[35]Gordon Chase and E. Reveal, **How to Manage in the Public Sector** (Reading, MA: Addison Wesley, 1983).

[36]Jerold H. Israel Y. Kamisar and W. LaFave, "Arrest, Search and Seizure," Ch. 3 in **Criminal Procedure and the Constitution: Leading Supreme Court Cases and Introductory Text** (St. Paul, MN: West, 1989), pp. 55-205.

[37]Steven R. Schlesinger, "Criminal Procedure in the Courtroom: The Exclusionary Rule," in James Q. Wilson, ed., **Crime and Public Policy**, (San Francisco: ICS Press, 1983), pp. 192-200.

[38]New South Wales incorporates this as an explicit value in the statement of their organizational values.

[39]James Q. Wilson, **Bureaucracy**, pp. 95-101.

[40]Peggy Wiehl, **William D. Ruckelshaus and the Environmental Protection Agency**, Kennedy School of Government Case No. C16-74-027 (Cambridge, MA: Harvard University, 1974).

Chapter 2. Defining the Police Mission

[1]Alfred D. Chandler, Jr., **Strategy and Structure: Chapters in the History of the American Industrial Enterprise** (Cambridge, MA: MIT Press, 1962).

[2]Egon Bittner, **The Functions of the Police in Modern Society** (Washington, DC: National Institute of Mental Health, 1970).

[3]For descriptions of police culture, see the novels of Joseph Wambaugh: **The Blue Knight** (Boston: Little, Brown, 1972) and **The New Centurions** (Boston: Little, Brown, 1970). See also Jonathan Rubenstein, **City Police** (New York: Farrar, Straus & Giroux, 1973); James McClure, **Cop World: Inside an American Police Force** (New York: Pantheon, 1984); Arthur Niederhofer, **Behind the Shield: The Police in Urban Society** (Garden City: Doubleday & Co., 1967).

[4]Mark H. Moore, R. Trojanowicz and G. Kelling, "Crime and Policing," **Perspectives on Policing**, No. 2 (Washington, DC: National Institute of Justice and Harvard University, June 1988).

[5]Peter K Manning, **The Narc's Game: Organizational and Informational Limits on Drug Law Enforcement** (Cambridge, MA: MIT Press, 1980); also Mark H. Moore, "Invisible Offenses: A Challenge to Minimally Intrusive Law Enforcement," in Gerald M. Caplan, **ABSCAM Ethics: Moral Issues and Deception in Law Enforcement** (Washington, DC: Police Foundation, 1983).

[6]Mary Ann Wycoff, C. Brown and R. Peterson, **Birmingham**

Anti-Robbery Unit: Evaluation Report, Draft 3 (Washington, DC: Police Foundation, March 1980); Malcolm K. Sparrow, M. Moore and D. Kennedy, **Beyond 911: A New Era for Policing** (New York: Basic Books, 1990); R. A. Bowers and J. McCullough, **Assessing the 'Sting': An Evaluation of the LEAA Property Crime Program** (Washington, DC: National Institute of Justice, 1983).

[7]Moore, "Invisible Offenses."

[8]Table 104, pp. 90-91, in **Criminal Victimization in the United States, 1987**, National Crime Survey Report No. NCJ-115524 (Washington, DC: U.S. Department of Justice, Bureau of Justice Statistics, June 1989).

[9] Alfred Blumstein, J. Cohen and D. Nagin, eds., **Deterrence and Incapacitation: Estimating the Effects of Criminal Sanctions on Crime Rates** (Washington, DC: National Academy of Sciences, 1978).

[10]Ibid.

[11]Lee Sechrest, S. White and E. Brown, eds., **The Rehabilitation of Criminal Offenders: Problems and Prospects**, The Committee on Research on Law Enforcement and Criminal Justice, National Research Council (Washington, DC: National Academy Press, 1979).

[12]William DeJong, **Project DARE: Teaching Kids to Say "No" to Drugs and Alcohol**, NIJ Reports/SNI 196 (Washington, DC: U.S. Department of Justice, March 1986).

[13]Ronald V. Clarke, "Situational Crime Prevention: Its Theoretical Basis and Practical Scope," in Michael Tonry and Norval Morris, eds., **Crime and Justice: An Annual Review of Research**, Vol. 4 (Chicago: University of Chicago Press, 1983), pp. 225-256.

[14]This example comes from New South Wales, Australia. Every Friday evening, a local station house was besieged by calls from elderly people that "gangs of marauding youth" were terrorizing their neighborhood. An investigation revealed that the teenagers were walking home from a skating rink that closed at that particular time. They had to walk home because the bus that picked them up and brought them to the rink, at the initiative of the owner of the rink, did not bring them home. The problem was solved when the owner of the rink was encouraged to

provide a bus home as well as to the rink. The authors are indebted to Inspector Christine Nixon of the New South Wales Police Department for this example.

[15]Vera Institute Report on Community Policing.

[16]John E. Eck and W. Spelman, **Problem Solving: Problem-Oriented Policing in Newport News** (Washington, DC: Police Executive Research Forum, 1987).

[17]Herman Goldstein, **Problem-Oriented Policing** (New York: McGraw-Hill, 1990).

[18]Eck and Spelman, **Problem Solving.**

[19]Ibid.

[20]Lawrence W. Sherman et al., **Repeat Calls to the Police in Minneapolis** (Washington, DC: Crime Control Institute, 1987).

[21]Wesley Skogan, "Fear of Crime and Neighborhood Change," in Albert J. Reiss, Jr. and Michael Tonry, **Crime and Justice: A Review of Research,** Vol. 8, **Communities and Crime** (Chicago: University of Chicago Press, 1986).

[22]Ibid, p. 210.

[23]Wesley G. Skogan and M.G. Maxfield, **Coping with Crime: Individual and Neighborhood Reactions** (Beverly Hills: Sage, 1981).

[24]Clifford D. Shearing and P. C. Stenning, "Private Security: Implications for Social Control," **Social Problems,** 30: 493-506, 1983.

[25]Anthony M. Pate, M. Wycoff, W. G. Skogan and L. W. Sherman, **Reducing Fear of Crime in Houston and Newark: A Summary Report** (Washington, DC: Police Foundation, 1986).

[26]U.S. Department of Health and Human Services, **Healthy People: The Surgeon General's Report on Health Promotion and Disease Prevention** (Washington, DC: U.S. Government Printing Office, 1979).

[27]George L. Kelling, **Kansas City Preventive Patrol Experiment: A**

Summary Report (Washington, DC: Police Foundation, 1974).

[28]Ibid.

[29]Kansas City Police Department, **Response Time Analysis** (Kansas City, MO: Kansas City Police Department, 1977).

[30]Peter W. Greenwood, J. Chaiken and J. Petersilia, **The Criminal Investigation Process** (Lexington, MA: D.C. Heath, 1977).

[31]William Spelman, M. Oshima and G. Kelling, **On the Competitive Enterprise of Ferreting Out Crime: The Nature of the Problems, the Capacity of the Police, and the Assessments of Victims,** Working Paper #87-05-01, Program in Criminal Justice Policy and Management, Kennedy School of Government (Cambridge, MA: Harvard University, June 1987).

[32]William Spelman and D. Brown, **Calling the Police: Citizen Reporting of Serious Crime** (Washington, DC: Police Executive Research Forum, 1982).

[33]Greenwood, Chaiken and Petersilia, **The Criminal Investigation Process.**

[34]William C. Cunningham and T. Taylor, **The Hallcrest Report: Private Security and Police in America** (Portland, OR: Chancellor Press, 1985).

[35]Ibid.

[36]Mary Ann Wycoff, **The Role of the Municipal Police: Research as a Prelude to Changing It** (Washington, DC: Police Foundation, 1982).

[37]Ibid.

[38]David M. Kennedy, **Neighborhood Policing in Los Angeles,** Kennedy School of Government Case No. C16-87-717.0 (Cambridge, MA: Harvard University, 1987).

[39]Herman Goldstein, **Policing a Free Society** (Cambridge, MA: Ballinger, 1977).

Chapter 3. Constituting Police Departments

[1]Philadelphia Police Study Task Force, **Philadelphia and Its Police: Toward a New Partnership** (Philadelphia: Philadelphia Police Department, 1987).

[2]Michael J. Kelly, **Police Chief Selection: A Handbook for Local Government** (Washington, DC: Police Foundation and International City Management Association, 1975).

[3]George Greisinger, J. Slovak and J. Molkup, **Civil Service Systems: Their Impact on Police Administration** (Washington, DC: U.S. Department of Justice, National Institute of Law Enforcement and Criminal Justice, 1979).

[4]David M. Kennedy, **Patrol Allocation in Portland, OR (B) PCAM in the City,** Kennedy School of Government Case No. C15-88-819.0 (Cambridge, MA: Harvard University 1988).

[5]Diana Gordon, **Police Guidelines,** Kennedy School of Government Case Nos. C14-75-024 and -024S (Cambridge, MA: Harvard University, 1975).

[6]Michael Avery and D. Rudovsky, **Police Misconduct—Law and Litigation,** 2nd ed. (New York: Clark Boardman, 1981).

[7]Lawrence W. Sherman "Reducing Police Gun Use: Critical Events, Administrative Policy and Organizational Change," in Maurice Punch, ed., **The Management and Control of Police Organizations** (Cambridge, MA: MIT Press, 1983), pp. 98-125.

[8]See David M. Kennedy, **Patrol Allocation in Portland, OR.**

[9]**Survey of Community Attitudes Toward Philadelphia Police: Final Report** (Philadelphia: Prepared for Philadelphia Police Study Task Force by National Analysts, September 1986).

[10] Ibid, p. 22.

[11]Ibid, p. 24.

[12] Harry P. Hatry, "Wrestling with Police Crime Control Productivity Measurement," in Joan L. Wolfe and J. Heaphy, eds. **Readings on Productivity in Policing,** (Washington, DC: Police Foundation, 1975).

[13]Donald Black, "The Social Organization of Arrest," Ch. 4 in his **The Manners and Customs of the Police** (New York: Academic Press, 1980), pp. 85-108.

[14]Hartford Institute of Criminal and Social Justice, **Civilian Review of the Police—The Experience of American Cities** (Hartford, CT: Hartford Institute, 1980).

[15]Malcolm K. Sparrow, M. Moore and D. Kennedy, **Beyond 911: A New Era for Policing** (New York: Basic Books, 1990).

[16]Peter Willmott, ed., **Policing and the Community** (London, Policy Studies Institute, 1987).

[17]Jack R. Greene and Stephen D. Mastrofsky, eds., **Community Policing: Rhetoric or Reality** (New York: Praeger, 1988) in general; in particular, Ch. 12, David H. Bayley, "Community Policing: A Report from the Devil's Advocate," pp. 225-237.

[18]For a specific example of this tactic, see Kennedy School of Government Cases: Sheila Jasanoff, **The Knapp Commission and Patrick Murphy (A), (B), and Sequel,** Kennedy School of Government Case Nos. C94-77-181, -182S, (Cambridge, MA: Harvard University, 1977). See also Mark H. Moore, "Police Leadership: The Impossible Dream," in Irwin Hargrove, ed., **Doing Impossible Jobs** (Lawrence, KS: University of Kansas Press, forthcoming).

Chapter 4. Managing Police Performance: Internal Organization and Control

[1]George L. Kelling and Mary Ann Wycoff, **The Dallas Experience: Vol. 1, Organizational Reform** (Washington, DC: Police Foundation, 1978).

[2]Lawrence W. Sherman, "Policing Communities: What Works?" in Albert J. Reiss, Jr. and Michael Tonry, **Communities and Crime, Vol. 8 of Crime and Justice: A Review of Research** (Chicago: University of Chicago Press, 1986), pp. 343-379.

[3]Henry Mintzberg, **The Structure of Organizations: A Synthesis of the Research** (Englewood Cliffs, NJ: Prentice-Hall, 1979).

[4]Alfred D. Chandler, Jr., **Strategy and Structure: Chapters in the History of the American Industrial Enterprise** (Cambridge, MA: MIT Press, 1962).

[5]Mintzberg, ibid.

[6]Michael Barzelay and Babak J. Armajani, "Managing State Government Operations: Changing Visions of Staff Agencies," **Journal of Police Analysis and Management,** forthcoming.

[7]Thomas J. Peters and Robert H. Waterman, Jr., "Simultaneous Loose-Tight Properties," Ch.12 in their **In Search of Excellence: Lessons from America's Best-Run Companies** (New York: Harper & Row, 1982), pp. 318-325.

[8]James Q. Wilson, **Varieties of Police Behavior** (Cambridge, MA: Harvard University Press, 1968), pp. 64-69.

[9]S.C. Tillinghast, "Role of the Team Manager," **Police Chief,** Vol. 43, No. 7 (July 1976), pp. 61-65.

[10]Samuel G. Chapman, "Personnel Management," Ch. 13 in Bernard R. Garmire, ed., **Local Government Public Management,** 2nd ed., published for Institute for Training in Municipal Administration (Washington, DC: International City Management Association, 1982), pp. 245-246.

[11]C. McCoy, "Enforcement Workshop--Affirmative Action in Police Organizations: Checklists for Supporting a Compelling State Interest" **Criminal Law Bulletin,** Vol. 20, No. 3 (1984), pp. 245-254.

[12]S.M. Cox and JD. Fitzgerald, **Police in Community Relations: Critical Issues** (Dubuque, IA: Brown, 1983).

[13]J.J. Prince, "Pilot Study to Select and Prepare Underprivileged Minorities and Women for Employment in Law Enforcement," **Journal of Police Science and Administration**, Vol.10, No. 3 (1982), pp. 350-356.

[14]Patricia Davis, "Suspected Drug Use Thins Ranks of Police Applicants; Fairfax Rejects Two-thirds of 1986 Group," **Washington Post**, September 28,1986, Al, col. 2.

[15]William Raspberry, "Smart Police" (Adam Walinsky, Jonathan Rubinstein proposal for Police Corps), **The Washington Post**, March 7, 1990, A27.

[16]Police Executive Research Forum, **The State of Police Education: Policy Direction for the 21st Century** (Washington, DC: Police Executive Research Forum, 1989).

[17]Michael Avery and David Rudovsky, **Police Misconduct: Law and Litigation**, 2nd ed. (New York: Clark Boardman, 1981).

[18]David L. Carter, Allen D. Sapp and Darrel Stephens, **The State of Police Education: Policy Direction for the 21st Century** (Washington, DC: Police Executive Research Forum, 1989), p. 110.

[19]Carter, Sapp and Stephens, **The State of Police Education.**

[20]Ibid.

[21]Donald C. Witham and Paul J. Watson, "The Role of the Law Enforcement Executive," **Journal of Police Science and Administration** (Spring 1983).

[22]Discussion with Quinn Mills, Professor of Management, Harvard Business School.

[23]James A.F. Stoner, **Management** (Englewood Cliffs, NJ: Prentice-Hall 1978), pp. 514-515. For an example of the application of these principles in other contexts, see **Executive Mobility: Thomas Winslow and the Navy's Rotation Policy**, Kennedy School of Government Case No. C15-88-834.0 (Cambridge, MA: Harvard University, 1990).

[24]John P. Kotter, **The General Managers** (New York: Free Press,

1982).

[25]Personal experience of Darrel Stephens.

[26]Frank J. Landry, **Performance Appraisal in Police Departments** (Washington, DC: Police Foundation, 1977).

[27]William Spelman, **Beyond Bean Counting: New Approaches for Managing Crime Data** (Washington, DC: Police Foundation, 1987).

[28]James Q. Wilson and Barbara Boland, "Crime," Ch. 4. in William Gorham and Nathan Glazer, **The Urban Predicament** (Washington DC: The Urban Institute, 1976), p. 225.

[29]Spelman, **Beyond Bean Counting.**

[30]George W. Greisinger, Jeffrey S. Slovak and Joseph J. Molkup, **Civil Service Systems: Their Impact on Police Administration** (Washington, DC: U.S. Department of Justice, National Institute of Law Enforcement and Criminal Justice, October 1979).

[31]Bernard L. Garmire, ed., **Local Government Police Management** p.25.

[32]Robert N. Anthony and Regina E. Herzlinger, **Management Control in Non-Profit Organizations**, rev. ed. (Homewood, IL: R.D. Irwin, 1980).

[33]David M. Kennedy, **Computer-Aided Police Dispatching in Houston, Texas,** Kennedy School of Government Case No. C16-90-985.0 (Cambridge, MA: Harvard University, 1990).

[34]Spelman, **Beyond Bean Counting.**

[35]On the distinction, see Anthony and Herzlinger, **Management Control in Non-Profit Organizations.**

[36]Joan Petersilia, "Influence of Research on Policing," in Roger G. Dunham and Geoffrey P. Alpert, eds., **Critical Issues in Policing Contemporary Readings** (Prospect Heights, IL: 1989), pp 230-247.

[37]National Committee for Injury Prevention and Control, **Injury**

Prevention: Meeting the Challenge, Supplement to American Journal of Preventive Medicine, Vol. 5, No. 3 (New York: Oxford, 1989).

[38]Philip J. Cook, "The Case of the Missing Victims: Gunshot Woundings in the National Crime Survey," Journal of Quantitative Criminology, Vol. 1, No. 1 (1985), pp. 91-102.

[39]Spelman, Beyond Bean Counting.

[40]See, for example, Peoria, Illinois, Advisory Committee on Police-Community Relations, Police Services: A Survey of Citizen Satisfaction and Police Services: A Survey of Youth Opinion (Peoria, IL: Advisory Committee, Feb. 1982 and Jan. 1983); Peoria, Illinois, Department of Planning and Zoning, Report: A Survey of East Bluff Residents Spring 1984 (Peoria, IL: City of Peoria, 1984).

[41]Lawrence W. Sherman, Police Corruption: A Sociological Perspective (New York: Anchor Books, 1974).

[42]Sheila Jasanoff, The Knapp Commission and Patrick Murphy (A), (B), and Sequel, Kennedy School of Government Case No. C94-77-181, 192, and 182S, (Cambridge, MA: Harvard University, 1980).

[43]Hartford Institute of Criminal and Social Justice, Civilian Review of the Police—the Experience of American Cities (Hartford, CT: Hartford Institute, 1980).

[44]In Sidney, Australia, there has been a vigorous political debate about continuing the ombudsman's office to oversee police activities. Personal experience of Mark Moore. See Mark Irving, "Officers May Be Corrupt: Ombudsman," Australian, Dec. 8, 1989.

[45]Candace McCoy, "Lawsuits Against Police: What Impact Do They Really Have?" in James J. Fyfe, ed., Police Management Today: Issues and Case Studies (Washington, DC: International City Management Association, 1985), pp. 55-64.

[46]Wayne W. Schmidt, "Section 1983 and the Changing Face of Police Management," Ch. 22 in William Geller, ed., Police Leadership in America: Crisis and Opportunity (New York: Praeger, 1985), pp. 226-236.

[47]Malcolm K Sparrow, Mark H. Moore and David M. Kennedy, **Beyond 911: A New Era for Policing** (New York: Basic Books, 1990).

Chapter 5. Leadership and the Future of Policing

[1]Samuel Walker, "Setting the Standards: The Efforts and Impact of Blue-Ribbon Commissions on the Police," Ch. 31 in William A. Geller, ed., **Police Leadership in America: Crisis and Opportunity**, (New York: Praeger, 1985), pp. 354-370.

[2]See, for example, Sheila Jasanoff, **The Knapp Commission and Patrick Murphy (A) (B), and Sequel**, Kennedy School of Government Case No. C94-77-181, 182, and 182S, (Cambridge, MA: Harvard University, 1977).

[3]Malcolm K. Sparrow, "Implementing Community Policing," **Perspectives on Policing**, No. 9 (Washington, DC: National Institute of Justice and Harvard University, Nov. 1988); see also Lee P. Brown, "Community Policing: A Practical Guide for Police Officials," **Perspectives on Policing**, No. 12 (Washington, DC: National Institute of Justice and Harvard University, Sept. 1989).

[4]Personal communication, George Lodge, Professor of Management, Harvard Business School with author.

[5]Mark H. Moore, "Police Leadership: The Impossible Dream," in Irwin Hargrove, ed., **Doing Impossible Jobs** (Lawrence, KS: University of Kansas Press, forthcoming).

[6]William C. Cunningham and T. Taylor, **The Hallcrest Report: Private Security and Police in America** (Portland, OR: Chancellor Press, 1985).

[7]Malcolm K. Sparrow, Mark Moore and David Kennedy, **Beyond 911: A New Era for Policing** (New York: Basic Books, 1990); David M. Kennedy, **Neighborhood Policing: The London Metropolitan Police Force**, Kennedy School of Government Case No. C15-87-770.0 (Cambridge, MA: Harvard University 1987); David M. Kennedy, **Neighborhood Policing in Los Angeles**, Kennedy School of Government Case No. C16-87-717-0 (Cambridge, MA: Harvard University, 1987); David M. Kennedy, **Fighting Fear in Baltimore County**, Kennedy School of Government Case No. C16-90-938.0 (Cambridge, MA: Harvard

University, 1990).

Police Executive Research Forum

The Police Executive Research Forum (PERF) is a national professional association of chief executives of large city, county and state police departments. PERF's purpose is to improve the delivery of police services and the effectiveness of crime control through several means:

- the exercise of strong national leadership;
- public debate of police and criminal justice issues;
- research and policy development; and
- the provision of vital management leadership services to police agencies.

PERF members are selected on the basis of their commitment to PERF's purpose and principles. The principles that guide the Police Executive Research Forum are:

- Research, experimentation and exchange of ideas through public discussion and debate are paths for development of a professional body of knowledge about policing;
- Substantial and purposeful academic study is a prerequisite for acquiring, understanding and adding to the body of knowledge of professional police management;
- Maintenance of the highest standards of ethics and integrity is imperative in the improvement of policing;
- The police must, within the limits of the law, be responsible and accountable to citizens as the ultimate source of police authority; and
- The principles embodied in the Constitution are the foundation of policing.